# HOW TO DATE A FOREIGNER ®

## A PROVEN FRAMEWORK TO HELP YOU
## NAVIGATE CULTURAL DIFFERENCES IN DATING

### SYLVIA HALTER

CULTUREZ PUBLISHING

LONDON

**Disclaimer:**

While all attempts have been made to verify the information provided in this publication, neither the author nor the publisher assumes any responsibility for errors, omissions, or contrary interpretations of the subject matter herein.

How to Date a Foreigner®
First Edition: Oct 2024.
Published by cultureZ Publishing, an imprint of cultureZ Ltd.
International House, 6 South Molton Street, London W1K 5QF, UK

cultureZ™ books may be purchased in bulk for business, educational, or promotional use. Please contact your local bookseller or email publishing@culturez.com

ISBN: 978-1-7394069-0-5 (hbk)
ISBN: 978-1-7394069-2-9 (ebk)

Cover photography from Adobe.com
Cover font: Metropolis by Chris Simpson
Editors: Mike Ettel, Julie Helliwell and Zsuzsanna Hegybíró

This is a work of nonfiction. Some names and identifying details have been changed.

# CONTENTS

*Acknowledgments* ............................................................. vii

*How to Read this Book* ...................................................... ix

## INTRODUCTION

1. My Story ........................................................................ 1

2. Challenges of Dating a Foreigner ................................. 11

3. The Building Blocks of Dating Cultures ....................... 15

   📝 What Is Your Dating Style? ................................... 21

4. How Many Dating Styles Exist and Why? .................... 23

## MINDSETS & BELIEFS

### Hierarchy (Linh & Scott)

5. Date to Find Love or Date to Marry? ........................... 33

6. How Does Hierarchy Affect Dating & Relationships? ......... 41

   6/1. What should you wear on a first date? ................... 46

   6/2. Do you have sex on the first date? ........................ 48

   6/3. Do you seek their friends' or parents' approval? ......... 50

   6/4. Is introducing the parents a BIG deal? ................... 52

   6/5. Do you move in together or live with his family? ......... 54

   6/6. Are you starting, or adding to your family? ............... 56

   6/7. Who is the most important person in your life? ......... 58

**Feelings** (Katerina & Jack)

7. Why Do Cultures Show or Hide Their Feelings? .................... 65

8. How Do Feelings Affect Dating & Relationships? ................ 73

   8/1. Who has the power? ......................................................... 76

   8/2. The male gaze ................................................................ 82

   8/3. How do they play "hard to get"? .................................... 88

   8/4. What is their dating "dilemma"? ..................................... 98

   8/5. How does it affect communication? ............................ 104

   8/6. What about dating etiquette? ....................................... 110

   8/7. Why do you feel rejected (When you're NOT)? ............. 120

   📝 Katerina & Jack on a Date – What went wrong? ............. 132

## DATING STYLES

### 9. ▓ Hugging Style

Explore dating in Anglo-Saxon countries like the UK, USA, Australia, as well as many Germanic and Northern-European countries.

   Countries where it is common ................................................. 145

   What are their mindsets & beliefs? ........................................ 146

   What are their dating stages? ................................................ 147

   When do they become official? ............................................. 149

   How long do they wait to say, "I love you"? ...................... 150

### 10. ◉ Kissing Style

Discover the dating culture of Eastern European, Mediterranean, Latin American, and many Sub-Saharan African countries.

   Countries where it is common ................................................. 153

   What are their mindsets & beliefs? ........................................ 155

   What are their dating stages? ................................................ 156

When do they become official? ............................................ 158

How long do they wait to say, "I love you"? ..................... 162

## 11. ⋈ Bowing Style

Gain insight into dating in beautiful exotic locations, such as China, Japan, Vietnam or Thailand.

Countries where it is common ..................................................... 167

What are their mindsets & beliefs? ......................................... 168

What are their dating stages? ..................................................... 169

When do they become official? ............................................ 173

How long do they wait to say, "I love you"? ..................... 174

## 12. ○ Traditional Style

See behind the curtains of some of the most traditional cultures in the world, like Iran, Qatar, India, and Bangladesh.

Countries where it is common ..................................................... 177

What are their mindsets & beliefs? ......................................... 178

What are their dating stages? ..................................................... 179

# COMPREHENSIVE OVERVIEW

13. Comparison of Dating Stages ........................................... 191

14. Crossover Between Dating Styles ................................... 195

15. Confusions & Misunderstandings ................................. 201

16. Conclusion: What Do You Bring to the Relationship? ..... 217

# APPENDIX

*Bibliography* .......................................................................................... *225*

# ACKNOWLEDGMENTS

Writing a book is a wild ride – exciting, but also super daunting. It's impossible to do it alone. So, I want to thank everyone who has helped me make it happen.

First and foremost, to my family. Thank you for being my rock throughout this journey and for all your love and support. I could not have done it without you. Special thanks to my mum, Brigitta, for putting everything aside to help me perfect this book and for all her amazing suggestions. Furthermore, I want to express my deepest gratitude to Zsuzsanna Hegybíró for offering her help as a highly experienced editor.

To a long-term client turned good friend, James Herbertson for giving me the final push I needed to actually write this book.

To my friend, Anita Advani, for saving this book from having a terrible title and for dragging me on the best hikes and getaways to protect my sanity.

To my friends Thu Nguyen, Vincent Murai, and Gui Perdrix, for all their amazing feedback and suggestions. This book would have a very different structure without Thu, would be a lot drier and more "educational" without Vincent, and would lack the summary comparison tables if it wasn't for Gui.

To my assistant, Maria Nosyk, for tirelessly supporting and believing in this book and being the best right-hand I could have wished for.

To my truly exceptional editors, Mike Ettel and Julie Helliwell, whose patience, positive personality, and concern for quality made them a joy to work with.

To my accountability partner and design thinking expert, Tracy Sharp, for helping me through the highs and lows of creating this book and the writing blocks I had along the way.

To the hundreds of contributors who shared their valuable knowledge and experiences in person or online. You have made this book what it is today, and I am honored to have worked with you all. Special thanks to:

Andrew Utman
Celie Scott
Chel Rogerson
Chris Globing
Chris Liew
Christy Van Der Wier
Gemma Ombuya
Jared Al-Jasser Morrison
Jenna Wylie
Katie Türsan
Katra Kwon
Kevin Park
Ksenia Khor
Leslie Betz
Loann Vu
Lucy Francis
Masha Vayman
Nhu Pham
Rimal Ahmad
Rownyn Curry
Simo El Asmar
Tom J. Colton

# HOW TO READ THIS BOOK

This book's mission is to teach you something that, to many people, comes very instinctively: dating in their own culture. However, it only comes to them naturally because they've spent the first 7-12 years of their life learning how to behave in their own environment. It took me nearly equally as long just to "decode" it. Therefore, I'd recommend reading it slowly: one or two chapters a day and letting it sink in. Don't beat yourself up for it if you can't remember all of it. Learning about dating cultures is like learning a new language. It takes time and practice.

## 1. Reading it from the beginning to the end

If you are reading it for the first time, you may want to skip all the gray boxes and pages marked as "Supplementary material." They will give you greater detail and deeper knowledge but are not essential to understanding the basics.

## 2. Reading it "backward"

If you have already met someone from another culture and need first-aid urgently, you can read this book "backward" – focusing on the person's dating style to start with. By doing this, you will skip learning about their culture's mindset and beliefs – which is essential to understand how they date. However, you can always get back to it once you have more time.

To read it backward: find the person's dating style (Hugging, Kissing, Bowing, or Traditional) based on the country they are from, and read the relevant chapters (9, 10, 11, or 12). If you are unsure, each dating style has a section titled "Countries where it is common", with a map to help you.

## 3. FREE Book Resources

Throughout the book you will find links to additional resources, such as videos or specific advice. They are not only very interesting but will also help you understand the topic even deeper. To access them, go to www.howtodateaforeigner.com/resources or scan the QR code next to them.

"Communication happens
on the listener's terms."

**Thomas Erikson**
Author of *Surrounded by Idiots*

# HOW TO DATE
## A
# FOREIGNER ®

# CHAPTER 1

# MY STORY

Left. . . left. . . left. . . I was killing time on a dating app during my short stay in London when his profile showed up:

. . . an athletic American, from San Francisco.

*Do not swipe right!* an internal voice warned me as my finger started pulling his picture to the right, indicating I liked him.

*Do NOT dare! He is a player – you can tell from the cocky look in his eyes!* the voice insisted.

Right. . . It's a match!

*What the heck are you doing?!*

Too late! I thought as a message popped up in my inbox:

"Want to have drinks tonight?"

We met up in a small wine bar near Notting Hill that evening and clicked instantly. Jokes and conversations flowed, and it felt so easy. Eventually, the bar had to close, but we weren't ready to say goodbye just yet. So, we found another one to continue until it was time to call it a night. He then walked me back to my hotel, gave me a kiss, and we said good night.

As I got back to my room, I messaged him to thank him for the great evening (exactly as I would in my culture), just to get his reply. . .

"You can come over."

*WHAAAT?!?! Who the hell does he think I am?!* I thought he was different. I was fuming, but for some annoying reason, I still liked him. So, I tried to squeeze my anger into a short three-character reply:

"???"

What I didn't know until several years later was that we had just had our first dating culture clash, and countless others were about to follow. Who would have thought that my extensive experience of having lived all over the world, from London to Paris, San Francisco, and Vietnam, and having had an American and then a British boyfriend for a combined total of 13 years – would not prepare me for the unwritten rules of American and British dating?

It turns out, according to American and British dating cultures, you should not message for a few days or else you can come across as too desperate, needy, or wanting to have sex.

So, as you can imagine, we were off to a great start. . . We managed to keep in touch for an entire year without ever going on a second date. But one thing really bothered me: I barely ever screwed up dates. Why now?! Why with him? Life didn't feel fair!

It was 2018, and I'd just gotten back to Europe after a couple of years of traveling around the world. By this time, I had been researching cultural differences in dating between Western and Asian cultures for two years. In fact, I only researched Asian dating customs, as I took it for granted that all Western dating is uniform. I never questioned whether Western dating cultures could have striking differences, too.

As much as he frustrated me back then, looking back now, he couldn't have come into my life at a more perfect time. Two months prior to meeting him, I was convinced I had dating cultures all figured out. I thought I had discovered everything and there was nothing else left. But he proved me wrong. This was the catalyst I needed to get back and dive deeper into my research, which eventually led me to discover most of the findings in this book.

## HOW DID IT ALL START?

Often, the people we meet or events that happen in our lives feel so insignificant at the time. Yet, years and years later, it's as if they were vital parts of a masterfully crafted plan all along. They shaped our lives in the most profound ways that end up defining us.

For me, one of these major life events happened on a flight to Las Vegas in December 2006. Thirty minutes from touchdown, our plane started shaking like a blender on steroids. The TV screens flickered away, and before I knew it, our flight attendant was sprinting down the aisle, screaming her lungs out in panic:

"Oh my God, oh my God! Let me get to my chair!"

A second later, the pilot turned on the loudspeaker. Instead of his usual 'Hi, it's the pilot speaking,' this time, with a trembling voice, he exclaimed:

"Everyone! Buckle up, buckle up!"

I always enjoyed flying and was never really bothered by turbulence. But this time, with the crew seemingly terrified, I realized that something was really not right.

It turns out we flew into a thundercloud. Luckily, I didn't know the severity of this until a decade later. The turbulence can be so extreme inside these clouds that it can tear an aircraft into pieces.

With every additional minute, descending felt like an eternity, but almost unbelievably, we landed safely.

However, it left me with the worst fear of flying for several years. Thus, I promised myself I would *never* fly again!

After I got back to Hungary, life was great. I got a job as a stockbroker trading on the New York Stock Exchange while I was still at university. They hired me after five rounds of interviews and out of 400 applicants. I attended university lectures from 9 a.m. – 2 p.m. and was working on the trading floor from 3 p.m. – 10 p.m. Most days, I got home at 11 p.m. and worked on my dissertation at weekends. It was extremely intense, but I loved it.

However, in 2008, in the middle of the financial crisis, I decided to quit and move to England. It seemed like a great idea at first, but there was one problem: I had the worst fear of flying. I had to find a solution. So, I started exploring my choices, from fear of flying courses to pilot classes, but their hefty price tag decided the outcome for the time being. I had no other option but to face my fear and force myself to fly, so this is what I did.

From then on, I took short flights to somewhere around Europe once a month. Initially, I was so afraid that I couldn't even hold a proper conversation with the person sitting next to me. But a "mere" two years and 50 flights later, I was comfortable with flying again – one of the most defining turning points of my life. Funnily enough, I was not just comfortable... Now, I had a serious travel bug. I wanted to explore; I wanted to see the world.

In 2016, exactly ten years after my flight to Las Vegas, I took the plunge and bought my first one-way ticket to start traveling around the world. If there was ever a time that felt like the hard work had paid off, that was it for me. Something that started as a terrifying flight experience made me think I would never fly again. However, it resulted in me jet-setting around the globe and even training for my pilot's license a few years later.

I had the time of my life:

I partied in a bomb shelter in Lebanon.

Went horse riding in Mongolia.

Walked in a forest full of fireflies in Taiwan—one of the most breath-taking places I've ever been to!

Woke up to the sound of wolves howling.

Took the Trans-Siberian Railway, the longest railway line in the world.

Learned to meditate from Monks.

Slept in a former prison in New Zealand (and got a really pretty mug shot!)

Went camel riding on the beach in Dubai.

Stayed with the Black Lolo hill tribe in Northern Vietnam.

Ended up in a music video in Taiwan,

. . . and met some of the coolest and most interesting people on the way.

This "slight turbulence," which in hindsight seemed like a little chance event, ended up influencing more than 15 years of my life. It made me travel around the globe and helped me discover different peoples' lives, cultures, and mentalities. It opened a whole new world.

*Searching for Souvenirs*

On a sunny afternoon, I was walking by the riverside in Da Nang, Vietnam – one of the very first places I traveled to. I was admiring their narrow "tube houses," busy coffee shops, and loud rush hour traffic with hundreds of motorbikes beeping to indicate their presence. It felt chaotic but, at the same time, captivating. I wanted to preserve a small piece of it. Something unique I could not find elsewhere. *What would I want?* I had just sold everything in the UK and rented out my apartment. The last thing I needed was more stuff.

That's when I passed a house where they had a wedding a few days earlier. Thinking about their celebration still put a huge smile on my face. Even though I hadn't known anyone, they dragged me in from the street all the way to their makeshift dance floor to go dancing with them. I was swept off my feet quite literally. They offered me food and drink without us even speaking each other's language. It was a truly memorable experience. Their culture was so different from what I was used to in the West.

I started to wonder: *how do they date?* Before I had a chance to find a more realistic souvenir, I knew this was what I wanted to "collect" on my travels – the peculiarities of dating cultures around the world. It was so different and unique, and something you couldn't just swipe your credit card for. This is how it all began, and over the years, it turned into a growing passion. I was slowly discovering a hidden world until finally, after two long years, it felt as if there was nothing else left to discover about dating. I couldn't find anything new that felt significant. I thought I was done.

THEN. . . life gave me a test: a date in London with the American guy, and I failed. Suddenly, it felt like all my years of research were worth nothing. *What was I missing?* I had to find the answer. For the next several years, I continued digging deeper into the topic until, finally, everything clicked. In this book, I will take you through it all. I will share my findings and the framework I came up with to help you navigate dating cultures worldwide.

Please note this book is not based on scientific research, but it does build on current knowledge in the research field. It is based on my findings from interviewing people around the world and, at times, my personal experiences. To ensure it is an enjoyable read for everyone, regardless of age and educational background, statistical insights are kept to the bare minimum.

Before we deep dive into it, let me share with you what I did and didn't do. The primary source of data for this book is the seven years of research I did between 2016-2023. I conducted interviews with over a hundred people in London, San Francisco, New Zealand, Hungary, Germany, Portugal, Vietnam, Sri Lanka, and Taiwan. In the beginning, these were very ordinary interviews as I didn't have any knowledge of dating cultures – I was in the dark. However, as I started to gain more and more awareness, these interviews got a lot deeper and more personal. For this reason, whenever people shared their experiences with me, I promised them anonymity. Consequently, following best practice in qualitative social science research, all the names of those whose stories I tell are pseudonyms.

To expand my reach beyond those cities, my assistant, Maria Nosyk, did an outstanding job helping me. She gathered information from all around the world through several Facebook groups. She collected hundreds of quality responses – many of which you will find throughout the book. Without her dedication, this book would not be where it is today. Huge thanks to Maria and everyone who contributed with their valuable feedback!

With the involvement of all these people, I managed to cover an extensive area of cultural differences in dating, but I did not cover everything. My research concentrated on heterosexual relationships only. However, as cross-cultural understanding is not gender-based, the concepts explained in this book also apply to LGBTQ+ relationships.

Additionally, most of the research I did focused on interviewing middle-class people around the world who went to college and were mostly in their 20s and 30s. Though I did interview and research the dating cultures of some extremely poverty-stricken tribes, they weren't my main focus. Therefore, variations related to class are not part of the book.

## Why Am I Writing this Book?

I had my fair share of mistakes and cultural misunderstandings; however, until now, I never realized our cultural differences caused them. I just blamed the person or simply concluded they were weird. Yet, once I started to understand cultures and shared my findings with my closest friends, one of them replied:

> "I wish I knew this 20 years ago!"

She was not alone . . . with the rise of global citizens, travelers, immigrants, and foreign exchange students, the number of international couples is constantly growing. According to the latest US Census Bureau Reports, 21 percent of married-couple households have at least one foreign-born spouse.[i]

Furthermore, the Migration Policy Institute's website highlights that: "As of mid-2020, the number of international migrants worldwide stood at 280.6 million (or 3.6 percent of the world's population), according to the most recent UN Population Division estimates."[ii] That's nearly the entire population of the USA!

Thus, finding and dating someone with a similar mindset is becoming increasingly challenging, despite the numerous dating apps out there. Many of us now grow up in one country but move a couple of times and settle in a third, fourth, or fifth, while all these cultures shape our personality.

Therefore, if you want to have a shot at making intercultural relationships work, it is important to understand how your prospective partner thinks. It will feel like having superpowers in your back pocket! But if you don't, get ready for a wild ride of never-ending miscommunication.

With this book, I hope I can help you avoid many misunderstandings and make intercultural relationships work for you.

So, what's in it for me?

I believe as our world becomes more connected, cross-cultural dating should be common knowledge. Yet most people do not know anything about it. Even those who have been in intercultural relationships for years or married to a foreigner are often unaware of how differently their partner thinks. I was one of them. So, I want to save as many people as possible from these mistakes.

There are two groups of people I want to provide value to.
Firstly, to those who feel a little lost in the world of international dating. Whether you've already met someone or are still looking for the one; if you're in desperate need of a "dating manual," this book is your ultimate guide. It is packed with all the information and insider tips you could ever need.

Secondly, to those who work in an international environment and want to understand or help people from other cultures.

Whether you work:

- In one-on-one as a matchmaker, relationship advisor, marriage counselor or psychologist
- In the travel industry meeting hundreds of people from all around the world on a daily basis
- With immigrants and foreign exchange students trying to help them integrate into their new environment
- Specializing in HR and Diversity, Equity, and Inclusion (DEI) at an international corporation.

In that case, this book will also give you a general understanding of cultures that will be useful for your professional life. And if you want to take it further, I have a partner program so you can become a licensed cross-cultural advisor or training provider.

So, in short, I teach everyone *How to Date a Foreigner,* and provide courses and licenses to those who want to make a career from it.

# CHAPTER 2

# CHALLENGES OF DATING A FOREIGNER

When I tell people I specialize in dating cultures and cross-cultural psychology, the conversation usually goes like this:

> "Wow, that's very interesting! How did you get into it?
> Tell me more about it!"

Then, a few minutes later, it usually takes a slight turn, just like it did with one of my long-term clients and now good friend, James. James is one of those few people I would go out of my way to meet up with whenever I am in London. We were catching up over dinner in a small but fully packed restaurant in one of London's hidden alleys when James challenged me:

> "But surely. . . if two people love each other, they will find a way."

Back then, I struggled to find a good example in response to James, but thanks to him encouraging me that evening to write this book, I now have plenty for you.

Several years ago, I met Adam – an educated and extremely well-traveled American English teacher in his late thirties. Ten years ago, he moved to China for work – just like many other foreigners who live in Asia. Shortly after, he fell in love with Yen – a very traditional Chinese woman from the countryside. They were happily in love and swiftly got married. However, over time, things started going downhill.

Adam recalls: "Our relationship was generally pretty good, as long as we did not have any disagreements. However, when we did, it went way out of control. Yen would never accept it if she did something wrong, and oftentimes, she even tried to turn it around and blame it on me. I consider myself to be a very calm and collected person, but when someone attacks me or blames me for things that were clearly their fault, I lose my shit. I am not going to let them get away with that. We would often go to sleep arguing and screaming at each other. Then you wake up the next day, all drained, and you continue because you never put an end to it. There was no resolution. Over the years, these arguments become more and more common to the point that you start forgetting the good times. It became so extremely tiring and draining that we ended up filing for divorce."

Interestingly, Adam's story is not unique. In fact, many other Western-Asian couples find disagreements and arguments especially difficult to handle.

## Why did their arguments escalate?

Adam grew up in the United States, where he was raised to admit his mistakes. In guilt-driven Western cultures, when you admit your mistake, people believe you are a step closer to learning from it and doing it better next time. On the other hand, his wife, Yen, grew up in China, where she was raised to avoid shame.

The terms "guilt" and "shame" are often used interchangeably, but there is a big difference between them.

Guilt comes from internally (from the self), and it is focused on your actions. It assumes you are naturally a good person, but you have done something wrong *on this one occasion* that you need to correct. It encourages you to improve it.

China Mike explains it in his blog post: "In the US, you can admit and apologize for your shortcomings and gain respect for your honest efforts to learn from the past" – including learning from your past failed relationships to do better next time. "Americans are generally forgiving if someone takes responsibility for their problems."[iii]

Shame, on the other hand, comes from externally – how you are viewed by others as a person. What you did reflects on your entire personality, and you are labeled a bad person. That becomes your identity.

For this reason, in Japan, many people don't get divorced. This is because a failed marriage (a huge mistake) could give them so much shame in society, that, for example, they might never get a promotion at work afterward. In shame-avoidant societies, even talking about past relationships is often taboo.

In his article on BetterHelp, William Drake describes the difference between shame vs. guilt very well:

Guilt is: "I did something wrong."
Shame is: "I am a bad person."[iv]

In guilt-driven Western cultures like Adam's, your honor and reputation go up the moment you admit your mistake. People view it as the person being honest and having integrity. They learned from their mistake, and they will do better next time.

On the contrary, in shame-avoidant Asian cultures like Yen's, admitting your mistake could ruin your reputation and destroy your life.

Reputation after admitting your mistake:

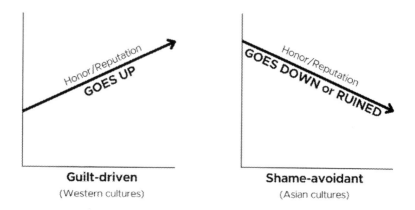

**Guilt-driven**
(Western cultures)

**Shame-avoidant**
(Asian cultures)

**Reputation after admitting your mistake**

So, why do our mindset differences escalate arguments?

When there is a disagreement between a Western and an Asian person, the Asian person usually tries to avoid shame. However, they don't realize that in the eyes of their Western partner, they ruin their own reputation by not admitting what they've done wrong. It is viewed as not having integrity.

In Adam's eyes, Yen was unwilling to acknowledge and learn from her own mistakes, which is considered a weak personality trait in the West. Therefore, by not admitting her mistake, Yen lost Adam's respect and ruined the relationship.

This can also play out the opposite way, with the Western person making and admitting their mistake and hence losing the respect of their Asian partner. Even though this is less likely to turn into a heated argument, it can still seriously ruin the relationship – often without the Western person realizing the issue.

Consequently, the biggest challenges of dating a foreigner come down to our mindset differences. This book will help you learn all about them.

# CHAPTER 3

# THE BUILDING BLOCKS OF DATING CULTURES

While sitting in a coffee shop in the buzzing city of Da Nang, Vietnam, I asked my local Vietnamese friend, called Thu:

"How do you date?"

Thu, a slender girl with shiny black hair, looked at me, perplexed, and replied, "We go to coffee shops." This was the moment when I realized that exploring my new field of interest was going to be a lot more complex than I thought.

What I wanted to know was: Tell me everything that is different in your dating culture from mine. However, how could she reply when she did not know anything about mine? Luckily, Thu was extremely kind and patient and took her time explaining her experience to me. She spent the entire evening trying to help me understand her dating culture, just for us to realize two hours later that even our definition of *dating* was different. You will see what those differences were later on in the book.

After our interesting conversation, I returned home thinking, *How could I have asked this question better? What did I truly want to know?* But honestly, the problem was that I did not even know what I wanted to know. I didn't know what I did not know.

So, let's look at the main areas we are going to cover and what we will learn in each: essentially, how this book is structured.

The simplest way to explain it is by using an analogy of a tree. To understand cultural differences in dating, we need to go back to the roots. Hence, we will start by looking at the differences between Western and Asian cultures. Even if you are not interested in dating someone from one or the other, still read it because cultures are not black and white. There will be areas later in the book where certain cultures in Western countries have a bit more Asian mentality or vice versa. Reading this section will help you navigate these differences.

We will then split Western and Asian countries further based on whether they show or hide their feelings. This will give us four groups, each representing a distinctively different dating style. We will refer to them by the way they greet each other: Hugging, Kissing, Bowing, and Traditional Style.

Finally, at the end of the book, we will look at some minor differences in dating among countries with the same dating style.

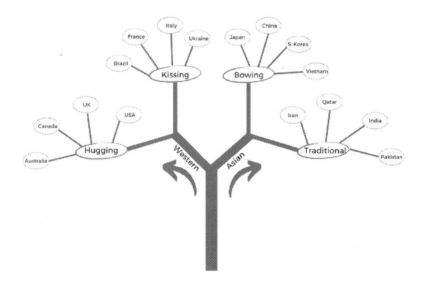

## DATING STYLES

When we talk about dating cultures, we talk about the dating culture of a specific country, for example, American dating culture, Canadian dating culture, or Australian dating culture.

Many countries share the same dating style – the US, Canada, and Australia, for instance. This is why you might find someone easy to date, even if they are from a different country. Although the dating cultures in these countries could vary slightly (you might find variations even within one country), they will not be *drastically* different. Dating in these countries will still feel familiar as they have the same dating style.

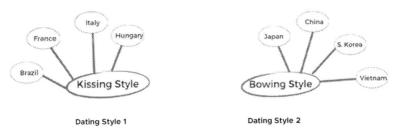

Dating Style 1                         Dating Style 2

Throughout the book, we are going to focus on dating styles. This will then help you understand dating cultures around the world much faster, as you will only need to learn a handful of styles.

Our dating style is a combination of our dating stages and our mindsets and beliefs.

**Dating Style = Dating Stages + Mindsets and Beliefs**

## DATING STAGES

Looking back now, when I asked Thu several years ago, I actually wanted to know about the Vietnamese stages of dating: the steps or the blueprint. This is what most people want to know when they talk about "How to Date a Foreigner" – they are thinking about the different dating stages.

## MINDSETS AND BELIEFS

For years and years, I thought all I needed to figure out were the dating stages. That was my dead end, where I got stuck in 2018. I could not have imagined that there was even more behind the scenes. It was something hidden deep under the surface that I had never even considered: how different our mindsets and beliefs are. How polar opposite we think and even behave.

Therefore, to get the essence of it much faster, we are going to dive into mindsets and beliefs first. Once you are familiar with how cultures think, understanding their dating stages will be a walk in the park.

### Why Do Dating Cultures Clash?

Dating someone with the same dating style will mostly let you stay in your comfort zone. It will come with some familiarity. Even if the person is from a different country, dating will feel easy as you have very similar mindsets and beliefs.

**Dating Style 1**
(Same Mindset)

**Dating someone with the same dating style**

Every dating style has its own distinct mindset and system of beliefs: a vastly different way of thinking and seeing the world.

Therefore, when you date outside of your dating style, it will challenge your comfort zone. This is why dating and relationships can feel frustrating as you are not on the same page, and often, you do not even realize it. This is where dating cultures clash.

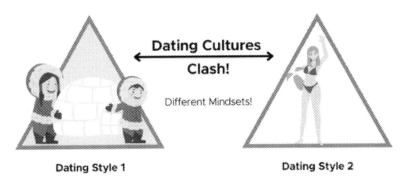

Dating Style 1       Dating Style 2

**Dating outside of your dating style**

You don't have to go all the way to China to experience some of these cultural differences. If I shake my head from side to side in most Western countries, you know I answered no. We are on the same page, just like having the same dating style. We both interpret my behavior the same way, so our communication is easy, and it flows.

However, if you visit Bulgaria, every horizontal head shake suddenly becomes a *yes*. Until you know this, communication can feel extremely difficult and frustrating, especially as English is not widely spoken. This is exactly what happens when you date outside of your dating style. The person will have an entirely different mindset and set of beliefs and will behave differently from what you expect (even if they have the same intentions).

Before I understood dating cultures, I often concluded Americans were players. Why? Because the behavior in American dating culture is precisely how a player would act in mine. You can try as hard as possible, but if you do not know you are sending the wrong signals, you will never stand a chance!

## PERSONALITY OR CULTURE?

Some say culture generalizes and stereotypes us rather than taking into consideration our individual personalities. Others say they have such strong characters that culture does not affect them. Of course, we all have unique personalities, but if you behave differently among your friends than around your family or colleagues, you are influenced by culture. These are our microcultures. We also have a macroculture that helps our country function as a society.

As Pellegrino Riccardi, a communications consultant, defines it in his TED talk,[v] "Culture is a system of behavior that helps us act in an *accepted* or *familiar* way." The emphasis is on accepted and familiar. Culture includes many visible and non-visible areas, including our dating style. It involves an unspoken language where our intentions are expressed through our behavior.

Even though we all have different personalities as individuals, culture makes our daily interactions simpler. It does not mean we are all the same, but understanding cross-cultural behavioral differences will make our lives easier.

When I first visited Bulgaria and asked a waitress for a coffee, she gave me a huge smile and shook her head horizontally. For a split second, I was totally lost. Had I only examined her actions, I might have concluded she was rude. However, viewing her behavior through her culture makes her friendly with good customer service skills.

Therefore, it is important to understand peoples' behaviors according to their culture, not ours, so we do not misjudge their personalities.

**EXERCISE**

## WHAT IS YOUR DATING STYLE?

Before we dive into dating cultures, I would like you to do a short exercise. Try to explain your dating style: your dating stages, mindset, and beliefs. Why do you behave the way you do? Try to be as detailed as possible.

It is not so easy, right?

By the end of this book, you might be amazed at how well you have gotten to know yourself. This book is not just a journey to help you learn about dating cultures but also to help you discover yourself.

Many countries share the same dating style – the US, Canada, and Australia, for instance. This is why you might find someone easy to date, even if they are from a different country.

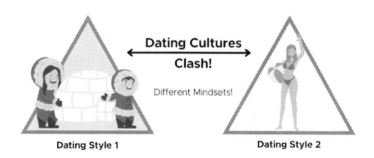

On the other hand, when you date outside of your dating style, the person will have an entirely different mindset & beliefs and will behave differently from what you expect (even if they have the same intentions). This is when dating cultures clash.

**Dating Styles = Dating Stages + Mindsets & Beliefs**

# CHAPTER 4

# HOW MANY DATING STYLES EXIST AND WHY?

I was three years into my challenging research exploring dating cultures, but I still felt in the dark.

Gradually, I started to recognize the following patterns, but I had no explanation for them:

- Why do many Americans, Canadians, or even people from New Zealand say they feel "vulnerable" when revealing their feelings?
- Why do some men "Chase women like they were a salesman?" (According to an Australian friend.)
- Why do many Americans think Europeans are "easy" and vice versa?
- Why do we find it easier to date people from certain cultures? How can we tell which ones those are?

This was when I came across a fascinating book from Professor Richard E. Nisbett, one of the world's most respected social psychologists: *The Geography of Thought: How Asians and Westerners Think Differently and Why.*[vi]

Mr. Nisbett explained how Western cultures could be traced back to ancient Greece and think analytically.

In contrast, East Asian cultures originated in ancient China and think holistically. *Was I not searching deeply enough?*

For the next few years, I buried myself in a mountain of books and research papers on cross-cultural psychology. I was on a mission to understand the roots of different societies.

I slowly realized that even though there are various dating cultures around the world, there are only four *distinctively* different styles. The rest are just like accents of languages. This is because there are gradual transitions across cultures.

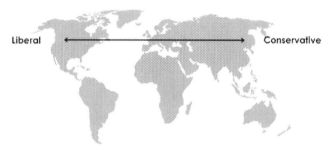

**Transitions between cultures**

As a general rule of thumb, the West is usually more liberal than the East (with a few exceptions like Australia and New Zealand). This transition happens on a big scale, just like it does on a small scale. On a global scale, the USA is the most liberal, while China is one of the most conservative (the Middle East is another exception).

We can see the same pattern on a smaller scale; Western Europe is a lot more liberal than Eastern Europe.
By the end of this book, you will be familiar with these transitions, plus you will find it easy to recognize and navigate the four different dating styles.

If you would like to know more about why these four different styles exist, I will give you a very brief history now. It will help you comprehend the cultures better, but it's not essential for you to understand this book. Therefore, if you prefer to skip this part and dive right into their mindsets, please continue with the next chapter.

---

Supplementary material

## WHERE OUR MODERN CULTURES CAME FROM

As we learned from Mr. Nisbett earlier, Western cultures can be traced back to ancient Greece, while East Asian ones originated in China. They are two of the oldest civilizations, and they had dramatically different views on life and approaches toward shaping their societies. Let's start by looking at the contrasting beliefs of these two ancient civilizations:

**Ancient Greek (the root of Western Cultures):**
They believed that "in order to flourish as a society, we must engage in truly *'civil'* discourse. We must learn to argue."[vii]
While their debates were civil (based on logic, credibility, and emotional appeal), the ultimate goal was to exchange ideas and to construct and put forth the strongest argument to win the debate.

**Ancient Chinese (the root of East Asian cultures):**
They believed in the harmony of mind and senses, man and nature. Their famous saying, which is still embraced today, is:

"A peaceful family will prosper (jiahe wanshi xing, 家和万事兴)."

In his article on *China's Traditional Cultural Values and National Identity,* Zhang Lihua explains that: "This benevolence, although based in familial ties, extends to friendships and social relationships, producing a full set of values."

It includes: *"justice, courtesy, wisdom, honesty, loyalty, self-discipline,* and *commitment."*[viii]

To avoid arguments, these cultures became hierarchical: where someone with a higher power (often the man or the elder) makes the decision.

As we can see, their approaches were the polar opposite of each other.

Ancient Greeks believed that progress comes with challenging each other's views and proving ours is superior for one reason or another.

Alternatively, the ancient Chinese believed progress comes with harmony. Opposing views and arguments hold it back.

Not surprisingly, many people today view American products and services as high quality (as their roots go back to the Ancient Greeks, they are constantly challenging each other to try and make things better).

In contrast, China is extremely fast and efficient at producing goods to the point that Western countries can't keep up. Their approach is: Don't question it; just do it!

*Religions and Philosophies:*

During the ancient civilizations, many philosophers started spreading their ideas and theories, and some still have an influence on our societies today.

At the same time, religions helped to spread these values and beliefs further. The main, and one of the oldest, is Orthodox (from the Greek orthodoxos, meaning: "of the right opinion"). As you can see, it's closely in line with the teachings of the Greek philosophers and the beliefs of ancient Greece: "We must learn to argue."

*From Religions to Dating Cultures*

As religions and philosophies spread throughout the world, they strongly influenced our values and culture.

At the beginning of the 11th century, relations between the East and West deteriorated until a formal split occurred in 1054, called the Great Schism. This created the two largest denominations in Christianity – the Roman Catholic and Eastern Orthodox faiths.

Another Reformation began in 1517 when a German monk called Martin Luther protested against the Catholic Church. His followers became known as Protestants (coming from the word protest). Many people and governments adopted the new Protestant ideas, while others remained faithful to the Catholic Church, leading to a split.

Because governments adopted these ideas, a lot of these religious values are now reflected in rules and legal systems.

One of the best examples of how religion influences society is Sharia Law, Islam's legal system. It is derived from the Quran - the sacred book of Islam, and the deeds and sayings of Prophet Muhammad: the Sunnah and Hadith.[ix]

An article from the BBC explains that Sharia law gives guidance and rules for every Muslim to follow so they can live their lives as per God's wishes. "Muslims may turn to a Sharia scholar for advice to ensure they act within the legal framework of their religion."[x]

On the other hand, in Western cultures, today the law is separate from religious values. The only connection we might still find is swearing an oath on the Bible at court.

An article on the American Atheist's website explains that:

"For a significant portion of the United States' history, many states did not permit non-believers to give testimony in court,"[xi] however, "Over time, state by state, those religious requirements began to fall away."[xii]

How legal systems in Western countries directly influence our mindsets and beliefs and hence our dating culture, we will get back to in a later chapter (titled "Why Do Cultures Show or Hide Their Feelings?").

MINDSETS &
BELIEFS

# HIERARCHY

How we date and what we expect from our prospective partner is a reflection of how we think: our *mindset and beliefs*.

They are strongly influenced by TWO key factors:

- how **hierarchical** our society is
- whether we show or hide our **feelings**

In the following chapters we will look at just how many different ways they affect dating and relationships – so that by the end of the book, you can recognize and navigate them. Let's start with hierarchy, which causes a big difference in mindsets between:

## Western - Asian cultures

# Linh & Scott

A few years ago, after having just arrived on the island of Hawaii from Japan, I ended up on a road trip with an American man in his thirties.

Halfway through our trip, I was curious to hear his perspective on dating in the US. Interestingly, he explained that many American men marry foreign women because American women are very individualistic, and foreign women are often more caring. *Hmm*, I thought . . . *the neighbor's grass is always greener!*

So, when I returned to Vietnam six months later, I was curious to hear what American men think about dating in Vietnam and generally in Asia. Do they really find it that much better?

I asked Scott, a man in his early 30s, to share his experience. Scott was originally from Los Angeles but had moved to Vietnam a year before I met him.

"How do you find dating in Vietnam?" I asked. "How is it compared to the US?"

"I'm still trying to navigate the dating field here," Scott said. "In one way, I love it – like I've never had a group of girls chasing me on the streets in the US! I feel like a celebrity here. Who wouldn't love it? As a Western man, I am getting so much attention here – it has never happened to me before.

"On the other hand, it can also be a bit frustrating because it is so different from what I am used to.

"Vietnamese women are very caring, but they also rely on their men a lot more. For example, in the US, I am used to always splitting the bill. However, in Vietnam, most women expect you to pay. It is very rare for them to offer to split it with you. I've met one girl who did, and it made me really appreciate it. Her name is Linh. She is my girlfriend now.

"Even though Linh is a bit Westernized, her family is very traditional. Most girls here live with their parents and have a curfew at night. They must be home by 10 pm! In the US, if a girl told me she lives with her parents, that would be such a turn-off for me. None of my friends live with their parents, but here, that is the norm. Curfew is a house rule, and Linh must follow it, too.

"For me, the early stages of dating were probably the most frustrating. Even just holding someone's hand is a big deal here. Forget about kissing a girl on the first date! When I started dating Linh, she seemed interested in me, but every time I tried to kiss her, she pulled away. I was really confused.

"Then my parents came to Vietnam, and I thought I am going to introduce them to each other. I invited Linh to join us for dinner, but she panicked. It felt like she didn't want to meet them. Turned out, she thought I wanted to get married, and she wasn't ready yet. Why would I want to get married after just a few months?

"So, dating definitely has its challenges here, but I am slowly learning the ropes of it."

Why were Linh and Scott having all these issues? In the following chapters, we will get to the root of it!

# CHAPTER 5

# DATE TO FIND LOVE OR DATE TO MARRY?

When it comes to dating, there is a key difference between Western and Asian cultures.

In the Western world, people search high and low for that magical connection that makes their heart skip a beat. It's all about finding that special someone, their one true love, who makes their world go round. But in Asian cultures, it's a whole different story - they date with one goal in mind: tying the knot. So, while Westerners are busy swiping and ghosting, Asians are out there, ready to march down the aisle.

When I first came across this difference several years ago, I honestly didn't understand it. I thought: *I date to marry too.*

However, in Western cultures, when we date, we are asking ourselves. "Do I want to be in a relationship with this person? Do I enjoy his/her company?"

On the contrary, in Asian cultures, the question is not simply, "Do I want to be in a relationship with this person?" but rather, "Would this person be a good husband or wife for me?"

So, while you're on a date with someone thinking it's all about chemistry and butterflies, your Asian date is secretly evaluating you as marriage material.

Interestingly, this difference has only existed for the past few decades, since people started to *date* in Asia.

Professor Irene Yung Park from the Department of Culture and Comparative Literature at Yonsei University explained that in Korea, the idea of "dating" has only gained popularity since the 1960s. It resulted from the introduction of the affective family model, when marriages became more based on love. Therefore, dating was the means of meeting someone and getting to know and love them. However, prior to the sixties, the Confucian family model was the norm, where marriage was a way to secure social and economic stability.[xiii]

Just like in South Korea, in many Asian countries, even though the concept of dating is now adopted from Western cultures, many of the Confucian values and beliefs are still kept.

As you will see shortly, this difference in mindset is very deep-rooted and will affect many areas when it comes to our dating life, such as:

- How you should dress for a date
- Whether you split the bill
- Views on having sex on the first date
- Whether you should seek her friends' or parents' approval

## WHY "DATE TO MARRY?"

When I finally understood the difference between dating to find love and dating to marry, I was on a motorbike tour in the mountains of Vietnam. Surrounded by endless rice fields between scenic mountains, my friends and I were having dinner with some members of the Hmong hill tribe. Our host explained that in their community, girls unofficially get married at the age of 13 or 14 and then legally get married at the age of 18. Boys inherit the land from their fathers, and when girls get married, they look after their husbands' land. So, men in this community get married to have someone help them with their land and raise their children. Meanwhile, girls get married for the perks of having a roof over their heads and food to eat (after cultivating their husband's land).

A week later, we returned to our normal lives in the city, and I quickly concluded this was the life of an extremely traditional hill tribe. However, part of me kept wondering whether our inheritance systems could have any influence on our dating goals and have any correlation to modern-day dating in the cities. To find my answer, I started researching the laws of different countries to learn more about gender equality in their legal system. I assumed in countries where both men and women inherit equally, they date to find love, whereas in countries where only one gender inherits, they date to marry. Yet, the laws I found often contradicted my hypothesis.

For instance, the law of Bangladesh states: "The Constitution grants women equal rights with men in all spheres of the State and of public life."[xiv]

I wasn't convinced. I've traveled and even lived in some of these countries, and in my experience, I saw that men and women were not equal. I had to research further. This was when I discovered customary laws, which confirmed the total opposite. My hypothesis was right.

Customary Law of Bangladesh: "Although Article 28[2] of the Constitution grants women equal rights with men 'in all spheres of the State and of public life,' it does not extend this principle to the private sphere."[xv]

This was when it started getting really interesting! I dug deep into the customary laws of countless countries and finally found my answer. The answer can be found hidden within every legal system. More precisely, it is found in each culture's inheritance system.

It holds one of the keys to the differences in our mindsets and beliefs.

## INHERITANCE SYSTEMS

One of the key differences between Linh and Scott is their cultures' inheritance systems. It strongly defines their mindset and dating culture.

We are either born into a culture where both genders inherit or where only one does. This strongly defines whether men and women are treated equally in society. Those who don't inherit, or do so only partially, have fewer opportunities and will always depend on others.

Therefore, in cultures where men and women inherit equally, like Scott's, they date to find love. Whereas in cultures like Linh's, where only one gender inherits, it causes a big gender gap between men and women. Hence, they date to marry.

To be able to navigate these cultural differences, we are going to use a system called the cultureZ™ spectrum. It is a tool I developed to be able to compare cultures. However, before we start using it, let me briefly explain where the name comes from.

Several years ago, I started playing with the idea of one day opening my international matchmaking agency. Though, one of my biggest headaches was: "How can I tell which cultures are compatible?"

I was sure there must be some tried and tested methods out there. However, the tools that existed (e.g., Hofstede's model of six dimensions or Erin Meyer's eight scales) compared cultures based on six to eight individual areas, whereas, I wanted to look at cultures as a whole. Eventually, I found that these individual "areas" are often the outcome of just two key factors: how hierarchical our society is and whether we show or hide our feelings. Therefore, after a lot of trial and error, I managed to organize cultures into a chessboard-looking "puzzle" that allowed me to compare their mentalities easily. Interestingly, cultures that were the most compatible with each other followed a "Z" shape.

This compatibility is what the "Z" stands for in cultureZ™.

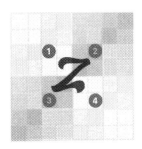

Hence, I later named this "chessboard" the cultureZ™ matrix – which is now my favorite tool for comparing cultures.

It can be used in romantic relationships between two people or for building highly successful corporate teams with hundreds or thousands of international employees.

However, understanding the basics is much easier if cultures are explained on a spectrum. Therefore, in this book, we are going to use the cultureZ™ spectrum, which, in many ways, is the simplified version of the cultureZ™ matrix.

Now imagine you could tell so many things about dating someone just by knowing two key factors about their culture. By the end of this book, you will be able to do so!

So, let's get back to the first key factor: hierarchy (which is caused by our inheritance system), and put the cultureZ™ spectrum in use. In Western countries where men and women inherit equally and therefore are legally equal in society, it is often hard to even imagine the opposite: life in conservative Muslim countries like Afghanistan. So, let's compare the two ends of the cultureZ™ spectrum to get an idea how hierarchy influences our everyday life. In the following chapters we will then dive into how it affects dating and relationships.

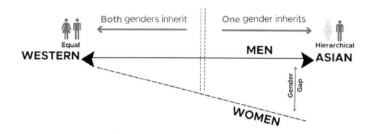

## MEN & WOMEN ARE LEGALLY EQUAL

Men and women are equal citizens, where women make their own decisions in all areas of life.

They have the right to study, work, choose their husband and get married without needing permission, travel alone, have bank accounts, mobile phones and properties to their own name as well as to be the guardians of their children.

## WOMEN HAVE A MALE GUARDIAN

Every woman is legally a minor and has to have a male guardian who makes decisions on her behalf, such as permits her to:

- Attend school
- Work (if she doesn't have permission, she is not allowed to work).
- Get married
- Apply for a passport, (or even be able to travel abroad without being accompanied by a guardian)
- Make medical decisions related to birth & pregnancy
- Women also cannot act as guardians to make decisions of their own children's lives.

Traditionally, a woman's male guardian from birth is her father and later on her husband.

**The bigger the gender gap, the more pride those with power have and the more respect they expect from the other gender.** In extreme cases, in very hierarchical societies, female family members could even be killed in so-called honor killings for damaging their guardian's pride (by bringing shame on him, e.g., by not being a virgin or by running away from their marriage).

Supplementary material

# INFLUENCE OF INHERITANCE

Most contemporary societies are, in practice, patriarchal. In these cultures, men hold the primary power.[xvi] But what about societies where *only one gender inherits*?

Some places are all about men. Property and fancy titles pass down through the male lineage.

In contrast, other corners of the world are all about women! In these matriarchal societies, it is the ladies who inherit. Property and titles pass down through the female lineage, leaving men wondering what happened to their manly inheritance.

Interestingly, one of the surviving matriarchies, the Mosuo women, lives in China (a strongly patriarchal society). However, there are also a few others, such as the Minangkabau people in Indonesia (the largest matriarchal society with approximately four million members), the Bribri people in Costa Rica, the Garo societies in India and Bangladesh, and there is even a rather new tribe, the Umoja village, in Kenya – a true no man's land, where men are banned.[xvii]

To help you see how much our inheritance system affects our culture and determines gender equality, let's look at some societies where only men inherit compared to where only women do. As surprising as it may sound, these practices are alive today in the 21st century.

Supplementary material

| Men inherit | Women inherit |
|---|---|
| • **Property is inherited by men**<br>"In Vietnam, son-preference is practiced in inheritance."... "Accordingly, most women do not claim their rights to inheritance."[xviii]<br><br>In Bangladesh, "women often surrender their right to property in exchange for the right to visit their parental home and seek their brothers' assistance in case of marital conflicts."[xix] | • **Property is inherited by women**<br>In the Garo community: "The wife is the owner of all of the property of a household and also acquires ownership of the assets earned by the husband." . . .<br>"After the death of the wife, the husband loses the right to stay and should leave the house; however, in practice, this custom is rarely applied."[xxv] |
| • **Man is the head of the household**<br>In Vietnam: "the man is the head of the household." . . . "A woman must unconditionally obey their husband and serve him and the children."[xx] | • **Mother is the most important person**<br>"According to a common belief by the Minangkabau people in Indonesia, the mother is the most important person in society."[xxvi] |
| • **Son preference is practiced**<br>"Sons are highly valued in Vietnam, while daughters are despised because they are traditionally considered valueless."[xxi] | • **Daughter preference is practiced**<br>In the Garo communities: "daughters are cared for more due to the fact that they are the ones who stay, while sons leave the home after marriage."[xxvii] |
| • **Boys get better education**<br>In Bangladesh: "Parents are more likely to spend on books and education for boys than they are for girls."[xxii] | • **Girls get better education**<br>"As a consequence [of daughter preference], literacy is also higher among Garo women."[xxviii] |
| • **Wife lives with husband's family**<br>In the Republic of Korea, "it is customary for newlywed couples to go to live with their husband's family."[xxiii] | • **Husband lives in the wife's house**<br>In the matriarchal Garo community in Bangladesh: "husbands live in the wife's house and engage in household work."[xxix] |
| • **Children take the father's name**<br>Among the Sinhalese (people native to Sri Lanka), "children take the father's name."[xxiv] | • **Children take the mother's name**<br>In the Khasi tribe, children take their mother's surname, not the father's.[xxx] |

# CHAPTER 6

# HOW DOES HIERARCHY AFFECT DATING & RELATIONSHIPS?

**In Western societies**, as both the son and daughter usually inherit equally, women have very similar financial stability in life to men. Therefore, as both genders have the same foundation, they *date to find love*. Men and women search for someone who gives them both emotional intimacy (love) and physical intimacy (sex).

**In Asian societies**, however, where properties and status are commonly passed from fathers to sons only, women start with a significant disadvantage in life. Men and women are not equal in society. These cultures are very hierarchical. If women don't get married, there is a high chance they will be left with nothing. For this reason, in these societies, it is important for them to marry a man who can financially look after them. Therefore, in these cultures, they *date with the aim (and often pressure) to marry*. Men search for women who will be great mothers to their children and good housewives (even if they now have a career). In contrast, women look for men who can provide them with financial security.

Let's look at a few examples from around the world. They will help you see this transition in our mindset and hierarchy.

## SWEDEN

*Swedish men don't expect women to be housewives, 'inferior,' or earn less money than men.*

*For example, it's also very natural for the typical Swedish man to take care of children, stay at home with the baby, and do things that are considered a 'woman's work' in some cultures. . . (Sofia)*

## ITALY

*Italians are traditional folks, and southerners are even more traditional (wives are frequently seen as home + cooking + kids).*

*So even when they speak out about being modern and accepting female emancipation, down under, inside, in the depths of its history, it has been influenced by a profoundly patriarchal way of living.[xxxi]*

## JAPAN

*A lot of men told me upfront about how much money they make and would ask what I expected.*

*This never happened in the States, so it was a shock. (Jennifer)*

Can you see the shift in how it went from gender equality (in Sweden) to men looking after women financially (in Japan)?

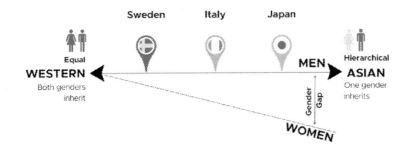

**Hierarchy on the cultureZ™ spectrum**

We can also see a similar trend when it comes to paying the bill:

A Saudi Arabian woman made a surprising discovery while attending one of my seminars. I was honored to be a guest speaker at Bayswater College in London, where I gave a seminar on cultural differences in dating.

The class was an amazing mix of international students from Colombia, Panama, Brazil to even Japan. To make it interactive, I asked students if they could explain to the group "How they date" in their culture. After some initial silence and shyness, a very interesting conversation erupted between two students.

A man in his twenties from Belgium explained that in his country, on a first date, the man takes the lucky woman to a restaurant. She can choose whatever her heart desires; he is not supposed to look at the price. The man pays. However, after being treated to a mouthwatering dinner, she is supposed to kiss Mr. Generous.

This was when a woman from Saudi Arabia joined the conversation with a complete shock on her face. However, it was not the kiss that left her outraged. She asked: "He pays only ONCE?" Still in disbelief, she added: "Men in my culture pay every time!"

Interestingly, despite never interviewing anyone specifically from Saudi Arabia, I could very confidently predict her problem, and by the end of this book, you will be able to do so, too.

With the help of my assistant Maria, we asked people from all around the world about several different topics and started seeing a very interesting pattern:

When it came to paying, Western cultures seem to lean more toward splitting the bill while in Asian cultures, men pay.

## GERMANY

> *If it's a date with a German man, do not expect that he will pay for you. You pay for your things, and he pays for his.* (Dag)

## MEXICO

In her blog post on the Spring Languages website, Paulisima, with self-irony, explains how it's rooted in society:

> *Even now, in 2021, a woman like me (you know, smart, independent, self-reliant, happy, feminist, fun-loving, modest)... even I melt down when my partner picks up the check in a restaurant, and they do it every time. . .* [xxxii]

## CHINA

A reader on Quora's website explains that:

> *Chinese people these days still take financial things very seriously. If he did not grow up in a Western culture and isn't paying for or does not offer to pay for anything, he is not serious.* [xxxiii]

Splitting the bill is not even typical among friends. They often insist on paying for shared meals or drinks and argue over the privilege of picking up the check.

However, this "pattern" wasn't only visible when it came to finances. There were notable trends in many areas.

So, let's look at how inheritance and, therefore, hierarchy in our society affect seven areas of our dating life:

1. What should you wear on a first date?
2. Do you have sex on the first date?
3. Do you seek their friends' or parents' approval?
4. Is introducing the parents a BIG deal?
5. Do you move in together or live with his family?
6. Are you starting or adding to your family?
7. Who is the most important person in your life?

We are going to look at three countries for each, ranging from close to equal to hierarchical, to see how different their mindsets are. By the end of this chapter, you will see how they are related, which will help us understand Linh's and Scott's challenges.

## 6/1. WHAT SHOULD YOU WEAR ON A FIRST DATE?

So, you managed to get a hot date? Congratulations! Now you are probably wondering: What should you wear? Don't worry, even if you do not follow the latest fashion, this section should give you some guidance:

### BRITAIN

> *It varies from person to person, but the dress code can be quite relaxed. Once, a Mancunian\* guy I dated arrived wearing shorts and a T-shirt. (Sarah)*

\*a person from Manchester, UK

### MEXICO

> *Appearance is important. It's true for both girls and guys. Thus, it's not OK to show up for the first date in jeans and a T-shirt. Most likely, a Mexican woman will choose high heels and a dress. A man is expected to look classy as well. (Julio)*

### SOUTH KOREA

> *Korean women will not date a badly dressed man. Status is extremely important here. Our place in social hierarchy significantly impacts our life. (Ho-Seok)*

So, people from countries with gender equality tend to dress more casually. Meanwhile, cultures with hierarchy dress up out of pride: to show respect and prove their status.

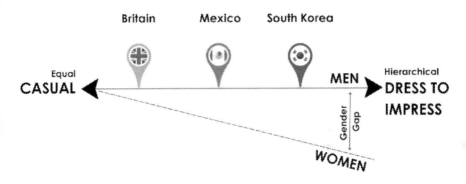

**What to wear on the first date**
**(based on the cultureZ™ spectrum)**

## 6/2. DO YOU HAVE SEX ON THE FIRST DATE?

Here comes the million-dollar question: do you have sex on a first date? Well, let's see what people think around the world:

### IRELAND

A YouTube commenter named johnc, explained that:

> *When we invite a woman out for a drink in Ireland, we'll go on a date, and possibly, there'll be a bit of 'you know what' afterwards, if both of you want it.*[xxxiv]

### SPAIN

Johnc, continues:

> *A Spanish woman sees going for a drink purely as socializing...*[xxxv]

### CHINA

> *People from mainland China are not as open about sex as Westerners, and public displays of affection are usually looked down on. Many Chinese women want to take things slowly. For us, the Western way of dating is uncultured and barbaric.*
>
> (Yichen)

In countries with gender equality, sex on the first date is accepted. Meanwhile, in countries with hierarchy, where virginity is often guarded, it is not.

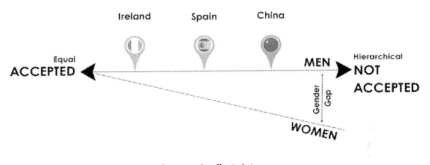

**Sex on the first date**
(based on the cultureZ™ spectrum)

Please note there are some Western countries that are slightly hierarchical (e.g., Spain), and hence, in many aspects, they behave more like hierarchical cultures. It will be clear which countries those are once we look at the four different dating styles.

## 6/3. DO YOU SEEK THEIR FRIENDS' OR PARENTS' APPROVAL?

My very first thought when I heard this was:

*Why would I need anyone's friends' approval?*

It turns out, in some countries, you do! So, let's look at whose approval you need to seek around the world:

### USA

> *Normally, in the US, once a girl likes you, you have to get their friends to like you. (Kevin)*

### MEXICO

> *In Mexico, you have to get her family to like you. So, be very polite, pick her up for the first few dates, and say 'Hi' to her mom. You might even be invited to have dinner with her parents so they can see you are a decent guy!* (Pedro)

### CHINA

A YouTube commenter named OE Match explained that:

> *Attracting a Chinese woman is about making her feel safe. If you can provide Anquangan "安全感" or security, both financially and emotionally, then she will love and respect you.*
>
> *Life in China was pretty tough at one point, so the older generations always wanted to own a house to feel secure. When you date a Chinese woman, you're essentially also dating her family, so if you can meet the requirements her family may have (a house and a stable job), you're going to make your girlfriend's life much simpler as her family has already accepted you.[xxxvi]*

In countries with equality, people seek their friends' approval, but in hierarchical ones, they look for parents' approval.

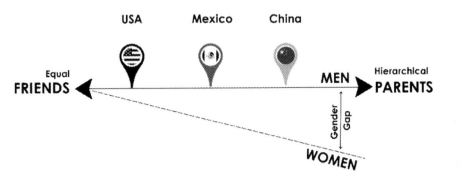

**Seeking friends' or parents' approval**
**(based on the cultureZ™ spectrum)**

Some Western countries (e.g., Mexico or my country, Hungary, just like Spain earlier) are slightly hierarchical. Hence, in this aspect, they behave more like hierarchical cultures. We will look at which countries those are when we talk about dating styles.

## 6/4. IS INTRODUCING THE PARENTS A BIG DEAL?

In some parts of the world, meeting the parents is a casual event, while in others, it is the most dreaded. Let's see who got lucky:

### GERMANY

*I'd say it's not so important. It's more like, 'Hey, Mum and Dad, here is the one person I'm investing a lot of time into at the moment. She is my girlfriend. Might be your future daughter-in-law or not. Who cares? I care about her.'* (Wulf)

### ITALY

An Italian man on Quora's website explains that:

*If Mom doesn't approve of her (even adult) child's relationship, things will get extremely uncomfortable!*[xxxvii]

### JAPAN

Chiaki Watanabe on Quora's website explains that:

*Until you get engaged, don't expect to meet his family. Even if you've been together for a while, don't ask to attend family events like weddings and funerals. It's frowned upon to let you do that until you're married, even if you are engaged, because these are strictly family events.* [xxxviii]

In the West, introducing the parents is not a big step. Meanwhile, in countries with hierarchy, it usually means you are getting married.

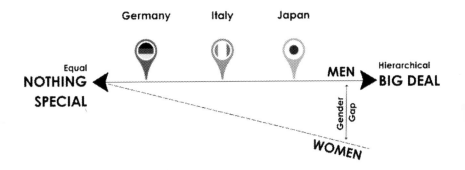

**Introducing the parents**
**(based on the cultureZ™ spectrum)**

If you recall, introducing the parents was one of Scott and Linh's challenges. Scott wanted to introduce Linh to his parents, because for him, coming from the US, it was a very casual meeting. However, being from the hierarchical Vietnam, Linh got cold feet thinking Scott wanted to get married.

 For tips for meeting the parents, scan the QR code or visit our website:
howtodateaforeigner.com/resources

## 6/5. DO YOU MOVE IN TOGETHER OR LIVE WITH HIS FAMILY?

Imagine that you've found the love of your life and are finally getting married. Like a dream come true! Except . . . just as you are about to walk down the aisle, you find out that after the wedding, you are moving in with your husband's family. His parents and grandparents. Oh, and his brother and wife live there with their newborn baby, too! Isn't it nice?

Well, it depends on what you are used to.

### UNITED KINGDOM

*In the UK most people move out from home rather early and often move in together with their partner before marriage. In fact, one of my classmates back in high school even had to pay rent at home once he turned 16 - encouraging him to move out. (Sue)*

### ITALY

*We move in together, but we often don't move out from our parents' home until we find the one. In fact, most Italians live with their parents even in their 30s. It is so common, we even have a name for it: bamboccioni (adult kids who live at home). (Giorgio)*

### VIETNAM

*Traditionally, the girl becomes part of her husband's family once she gets married. So, after marriage, we leave our family home and move in with our husband and his family. (Nguyen)*

In Western cultures, once the couple gets married (or often earlier), they move out of their parents' home and move in with their partner.

On the contrary, in Asian cultures, traditionally, the wife moves in with her husband's family. She looks after his parents and grandparents – cleans and cooks for them.

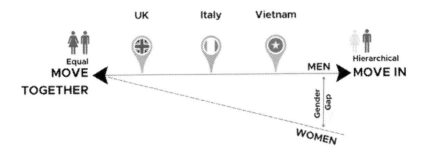

**Do you move together or move in?**

**(based on the cultureZ™ spectrum)**

## 6/6. ARE YOU STARTING OR ADDING TO YOUR FAMILY?

### AUSTRALIA

*Once we get married, we start our own family. (Charlotte)*

### VIETNAM

*When we date, we are looking for a person we can grow the family with. (Anh)*

### INDIA

Kanan on Quora's website explains it very clearly:

*In Western cultures, marriage is about starting your own family. In the Indian context, it is more about adding to your [existing] family.[xxxix]*

Kanan then explains it further:

When it comes to choosing a partner, Indians think about the entire family. It is not just "Do I like the person?" but more about "Do I like their family? Do I like their culture?" Someone could be totally compatible with you, but if their family is not, eventually problems will creep in.

Until Kanan highlighted this difference, I always thought people in Vietnam were looking for someone they would be happy to have children with. This is because in Western cultures, starting a family and "growing a family" means having children.

However, in Asian cultures, where traditionally, the woman moves in with her husband's family after marriage, he wants to ensure his wife will get on well with his parents and grandparents.

Therefore, the big difference is that in Western cultures, people are looking for a partner who is suitable for *them* and with whom, one day, they can potentially start their own family together.

On the other hand, in Asian cultures, spouses marry into the family, and by marrying, people add to their biological family. Therefore, they are looking for a person who is suitable not only for themselves but also for their *existing family*.

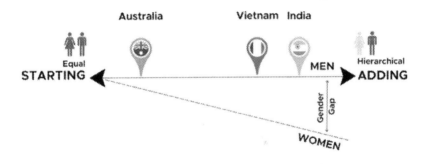

**Starting or adding to your existing family?**
**(based on the cultureZ™ spectrum)**

## 6/7. WHO IS THE MOST IMPORTANT PERSON IN YOUR LIFE?

*"If both your mum and your wife fell into the water, who would you save?"* In China, if you say your wife, it is the wrong answer!

This is something to be aware of, as it can stir up some serious relationship dramas. Not only if you make your partner your highest priority, and you are not theirs, but also if they want to bring their elderly parents into your love nest while you are busy planning to send them off to a care home. So, let's look at the differences in our mindset around the world:

### HUNGARY

*The most important person (especially after marriage) is your significant other. Of course, you will always be there for your parents, but your partner will be your highest priority.* (Andrea)

### INDIA

Ismenia Ujar explains it on Quora's website that Indian men behave like they are modern and considerate when they are on dates. However, when their family is around, they totally change.

*"Parents are gods for Indian sons."*
*"Indian men expect you to treat their family like gold."*[xl]

*Even the High Court in India ruled that a man can seek divorce if his wife tries to separate him from his parents.*

In Western countries, once people get married (regardless of gender), the most important person in their life will be their significant other. Their partner comes before everyone else.

On the other hand, in Asian cultures – especially for men (who have filial piety* duties) – it is their parents (often their mum).

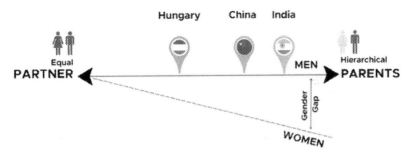

**Who is the most important person in your life?**
**(based on the cultureZ™ spectrum)**

*"Filial piety is the attitude of obedience, devotion and care toward one's parents and elder family members."[xli]

Whether our culture is equal or hierarchical affects every area of our dating life, from choosing activities to the language we use:

## SOUTH KOREA

> *Korean women want to date leaders, who take control. So don't ask where she wants to go. She wants you to decide.*
>
> *Despite Korea being a developed country, it's still very patriarchal. (Shi Woo)*

A casual way of talking is NOT OK in Korea on the first date. You should respect hierarchy even in your language:

> *If you're speaking Korean and they want to use 반말*
>
> *['informal speech' – a form that you use to speak with younger people or close friends] right away – red flag!!!! (Hae-Won)*
>
> *It's not respectful. They wouldn't do it to a Korean girl, so they shouldn't do it to you. (Kyung-Mi)*

Doug from the USA summarized this hierarchical difference simply: "In Mexico, I'm a man; in America, I'm a boyfriend."

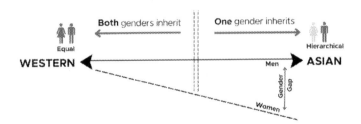

## summary

**Both** genders inherit → Equal — WESTERN

**One** gender inherits → Hierarchical — ASIAN

Men — Gender Gap — Women

| Western (Equal) | Asian (Hierarchical) |
|---|---|
| • Men and women inherit equally | • Only one gender inherits |
| • **Date to find love** | • **Date to marry** |
| • Get his/her **friends' approval** | • Get his/her **parents' approval** |
| • They look for a partner who they can **be a good team** with (e.g. has a similar education and goals in life) | • They look for a partner who **looks after them** well:<br> ○ Women look for a husband who can look after them financially<br> ○ Men look for a wife who will be a great housewife. |
| • **Women don't have a curfew** at night | • **Women often have a curfew** to get home by a certain hour at night - their purity (virginity) is often a prerequisite for marriage. Curfew is a way to protect it. |
| • They **split the bill equally**, even on the first date (especially in masculine cultures - which we will look at in the next chapter) | • **Men often pay on the first date** (or on later dates as well) to show their generosity and ability to provide financial security. |
| • They **split the housework equally** | • They usually **don't split the housework.** It is the woman's job. |
| • They **split the work of raising their children** equally. | • They usually **don't split the work of raising their children.** It is the woman's job. |
| • Women often find **strong men masculine** because they can physically protect them. | • Women often find **generous men masculine** because they can provide them with financial security |
| • **Love is usually a prerequisite for marriage** and having children. | • **Love is not a prerequisite for marriage** and having children. If lucky, it develops after marriage - though times are slowly changing. |

How to Date a Foreigner

# FEELINGS

After **hierarchy**, the second most important cultural factor influencing our mindset and beliefs is whether we show or hide our **feelings**. This makes a particularly big difference in dating between:

## Western cultures

Let's look at just how many ways it affects dating and relationships.

STORY OF

# Katerina & Jack

Several years ago, I met Katerina, a foreign exchange student from Bulgaria. She had always been pretty confident when it came to dating until she fell for Jack from Vancouver, Canada . . .who turned her world upside down.

Katerina explains:

"Very early into our date, Jack started telling me about his career and education, which turned into a half-an-hour-long conversation.

However, in my culture, we don't talk about these areas as much during the early parts of dating – especially not on a first date. Our dates are more about finding common interests and having fun.

Anyway. . . overall, we had a really nice date, but then Jack asked me if I wanted to go over to his place. It felt so disrespectful! Why ruin it like that?"

However, the problems didn't end here. Katerina recalls:

"After we said goodbye, he disappeared from the face of the earth. I hadn't heard from him for days – even though he clearly seemed interested. In my culture, when men are interested, they are very forward and communicative, but Jack really confused me. I liked him, but because he didn't chase me, I started questioning whether I had impressed him enough. I started to feel I had to prove myself. However, the more I reached out to him, the more rejected I felt."

Katerina's story probably leaves you wondering: maybe Katerina just wasn't Jack's type. If she was, he would have clearly made more effort. She should have just accepted it and moved on.

On the surface, I couldn't agree with you more. However, it is important to understand where they were both coming from before we jump to conclusions. Therefore, in the following chapters, we will dive into understanding Katerina's and Jack's mindsets and their strikingly polar opposite approaches to dating.

# CHAPTER 7

# WHY DO CULTURES SHOW OR HIDE THEIR FEELINGS

Katerina and Jack both came from a Western culture – where men and women inherit equally. Therefore, if *hierarchy* wasn't the root cause of their issues, what was it?

To get answers to these questions (and many more), let's take it a step further and divide our cultureZ™ spectrum based on whether cultures show or hide their feelings. These will be the foundations of the four distinctively different dating styles that we will look at later in the book. They will also help us understand exactly what happened between Katerina and Jack.

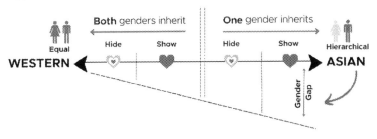

**Feelings on the cultureZ™ spectrum**

According to Richard D. Lewis – one of the most respected social psychologists – some cultures hide their feelings while others show them. In this book, we are going to combine Richard D. Lewis's findings with Geert Hofstede's.

Geert Hofstede, a social psychologist, was one of the first to define cultures by gendered traits. His theory says that cultures can be categorized by gender based on what motivates them: individual achievement – wanting to be the best (masculine culture) or liking what they do (feminine culture).[xlii]

Therefore, in this book, we are going to refer to cultures as:

> • **Masculine:** success- and money-oriented and tending to *hide their feelings* (e.g., the UK, USA, Australia, Germany)
> • **Feminine:** people-oriented and tending to *show their feelings* (e.g., Mexico, Brazil, France, Italy, Hungary, Ukraine)

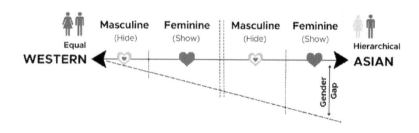

**Masculine and Feminine cultures on the cultureZ™ spectrum**

If you are wondering, "Why would people hide their feelings?" or the exact opposite, "Why would they ever show them?" We are going to look at that now. However, this is not essential to understanding the book. Therefore, if you prefer to skip it, you can continue with the next chapter: *How do feelings affect dating & relationships?*

Supplementary material

# WHY ARE CULTURES MASCULINE OR FEMININE?

## *Masculine cultures*

Our values are strongly influenced by what opportunities we have in life. Countries where starting a business is easy tend to be success- and money-oriented (masculine cultures). As we know, masculine cultures hide their feelings, but Western and Asian cultures do it for different reasons:

- **Western cultures:** If you recall, Western cultures trace their roots back to Ancient Greece, where their philosophy was: "Victory is the goal." However, in these extremely competitive societies (e.g., the USA), people can be very opinionated and judgemental. Judging others is often a tool to prove their own competence. Even in private, when they need a supporting shoulder, they still feel the weight of judgment hanging over their heads. Thus, to protect themselves from being vulnerable, they hide their feelings.

> *Germans, in my experience, are quite direct and cold. English people and Americans get on with them quite well. (Karl)*

- **Asian cultures,** on the other hand, originate from Ancient China. Their philosophy is: "A peaceful family will prosper." Therefore, they focus on money and success THROUGH relationships. In these cultures, you can only succeed if you have connections (e.g., you need an introduction to get a job).

When someone you care about does something upsetting, hiding your annoyance will save the situation from escalating into a conflict. Therefore, these cultures hide their feelings to protect their relationships, even though they are success- and money-oriented.

> *I believe Korean-Japanese values and education prevent men from being romantic as obedience and silence are constantly enforced at home and at school. I'm focused on working and problem-solving, but romance feels awkward and uncomfortable to me.*
> (Joon-Sik)

*Feminine cultures:*

In contrast, countries where opening businesses is difficult or borrowing money is expensive (due to high interest rates), are lifestyle- and people-oriented. In these countries, the barriers to making money are so high that people focus on having a good time instead.

- **People-oriented Western cultures** (e.g., Italy, Mexico, or my country, Hungary), prioritize their relationships and they show their feelings. In these cultures, when people judge, they usually do it purely as constructive criticism to help the other person become a better version of themselves. They are focused on helping the other person improve rather than proving their own competence (by potentially judging the other). In these cultures, private situations when the person needs a supporting shoulder are automatically considered a "safe space" (without verbalizing it) to protect the relationship.

Max explains:

It can be a bit too intense for people from Germanic or Anglo-Saxon cultures. With Italian women, there is never a dull moment, which can be as good as bad. *One second, you're passionately making out, and the next, she's really, really mad at you for doing something silly, like looking at another girl in the street.*

Max thinks Italian girls reflect a lot of their culture: which is to show their feelings. They will tell you when they're happy as well as when they're not.[xliii]

Let's compare the opportunities masculine and feminine cultures have when they want to succeed:

**Ease of doing business rank 2019**

**Ease of doing business rank 2019**[xliv]

Here we can see countries' ease of doing business rank (1 = most business-friendly regulations) – The World Bank

According to the World Bank, the UK is ranked 8, while my home country of Hungary is ranked 52. Let's compare how much it costs to set up a limited company (based on 2022 prices).

**United Kingdom (masculine/money-oriented culture):**
- Lawyer: £0 (you can set up a company yourself)
- Company registration fee: £12 (online)
- Shareholder's capital: £1 (minimum)
- **Total: £13** and takes 24hrs if done online

**Hungary (feminine/people-oriented culture):**
- Lawyer (with duty): approx. 130,000 HUF (~£271)
- Company registration fee: 100,000 HUF (~£208)
- Shareholder's capital: 3,000,000 HUF (~£6,250)
- **Total: 3,230,000 HUF (~£6,730)** and it can take weeks

(In some developing countries like Cameroon in Africa, even just getting a new ID card can take a year. By the time it arrives, you probably need a new picture!)
But let's stick with the UK and Hungary. . .

For ease of comparison, let's use McDonald's wages (2022):
In the UK, a Catering Assistant at McDonald's earns £7.43/hour. Therefore, you can set up a company just by working 2 hrs.

In Hungary, the same worker earns 2,000 HUF, meaning you have to work 1615 hours (9 months!) just to set up a limited company. This is what I mean by a barrier to making money.

In some countries, this barrier is so high that it demotivates people from working. They would much rather work the minimum to get by and spend the rest of their time with their family and friends. Therefore, these societies became people-oriented (feminine cultures).

The other important factor is banks' lending interest rates. It's hard to make money without having access to money.

**Lending interest rate (%) 2021**

**Lending interest rate 2021**[xlv]
(Interest rates ranging between 0-48%. Lighter countries on the image have lower interest rates.)

Countries such as the UK, USA, Canada, Australia, Germany, and Scandinavian countries are money-oriented. As you can see, they have much lower interest rates than the lifestyle- and people-oriented Eastern European, Mediterranean, African, and Latin-American countries.

**Our countries' rules and legal systems shape our mindsets and beliefs.**

# CHAPTER 8

# HOW DO FEELINGS AFFECT DATING & RELATIONSHIPS?

*In other words, what difference does it make in dating whether your culture is masculine or feminine?*

Quite a big difference, especially in Western cultures!

In Asian societies where only one gender inherits, the privileged gender starts with a significant advantage in life compared to the other gender in their society. They have the power as it comes with inheritance. Therefore, in these societies, marriage is an "exchange contract": The woman bears the man's children in exchange for financial security.

On the other hand, in Western cultures like Katerina's and Jack's, where men and women inherit equally, inheritance doesn't determine who has the power. This is where the differences between masculine and feminine cultures come into play. It determines who has the power – which is essential to understand how they date. Therefore, in this part of the book, we will focus purely on masculine and feminine cultures in the West, where the dating dynamics are extremely different from Asian societies. In Western societies where women have similar finances as men do, marriage is not based on exchange. In these cultures, men and women look for love and physical intimacy (sex). It's not an exchange, as each gender gives both.

As masculine and feminine cultures are polar opposites of each other, even our approach to something as simple as how we try to impress our date is different. Even though Katerina wasn't aware of it, she did notice it. If you recall, she explained how Jack was telling her about his career and education to a great extent, while she wasn't used to talking about these on a first date.
This is because:

> **Masculine cultures** like the USA, where Jack is from, focus on success and money and try to *impress with their achievements* (job, money, education).
>
> Whereas **feminine cultures**, like Bulgaria, where Katerina is from, focus on people and lifestyles and try to impress with their personalities (including their manners). On the contrary, trying to impress with your achievements in feminine cultures is often viewed as bragging.

### SPAIN

Sebastiaan Brouwer from the Netherlands who now lives in Spain noticed this difference also. He explains that:

> *Spanish people don't talk about job/money because they are more interested in you as a person. Generally, in the Netherlands, these conversations are often an attempt to judge or categorize the person. Whereas in Spain, they don't care. If they do ask about your job, it's only because they want to get to know you. Whether you are a company director or a street cleaner, they will like you the same, as long as you are a nice person.* [xlvi]

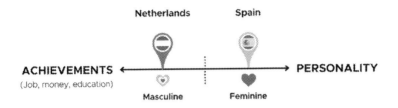

However, there is a lot more to it. So, let's look at how showing or hiding our feelings affects seven areas of dating life:

1. Who has the power?
2. The male gaze
3. Playing hard to get
4. The dating "dilemma"
5. Communication
6. Dating etiquette
7. Feeling rejected (when you're NOT)

They will help us understand Katerina's and Jack's problems.

## 8/1. WHO HAS THE POWER?

*Sexy or Sexist?*

Right in the midst of trying to figure out dating cultures, I came across the Netflix series Emily in Paris.[xlvii]

The story is about a young girl, Emily, an American marketing exec. After getting her dream job in Paris, she moves across the world to start her adventurous new life. Culture clashes, especially with her new French boss, Sylvie Grateau, become part of her daily life.

Sylvie is stylish, confident, and wise, and she lives by her own rules. However, she clearly has it in for Emily. She doesn't like the attention that the young Emily is getting from Antoine, a long-term client, with whom Sylvie is having an affair. Whether she likes it or not, Sylvie has to put up with it as they are attending a video shoot that Antoine's perfume company is paying for.

They are watching a rough cut of Antoine's commercial, featuring an attractive woman who is walking across a bridge naked while getting all the male attention. The French love it, but Emily is shocked and borderline at a loss for words. She asks:

"Whose dream is it anyway — the men's or the woman's?"

She claims the advertisement is sexist, but Antoine says it's the woman's dream to be admired and desired by men. This is when Emily highlights that the problem is the male gaze.

Sylvie is now clearly getting annoyed, but Emily wants to make a point. She is worried that American women won't respond to it.

As the conversation is turning extremely uncomfortable, they stop the shoot to have some lunch. Antoine is curious as to what is wrong with the male gaze.

Emily explains, "The men are objectifying her. They have the power." But Antoine replies, "No, she has the power. Because she is beautiful, and she is naked, which gives her more power."

According to Emily, in the States, it could come off as politically incorrect, and she looks at Sylvie to see whether she knows what she means.

Sylvie joins the conversation. "Cherie, I'm a woman; I'm not a feminist. But regardless, it's her dream to walk naked across the Point Alexandre III and have men want her. Maybe it's not your dream, Emily, but that's her dream."

Emily says she just wants to protect the brand.

Antoine adds, "And we need to protect ourselves from the morality police. Desire doesn't mean lack of respect. In fact, quite the opposite. It is a sign of respect."

Then Antoine looks at Sylvie and continues with, "There is no bigger compliment."

They have very different views, but in the end, they all agree on one thing: it's open to interpretation.

## *Who Has the Power?*

After watching this part of Emily in Paris, I had to rewind it a few times. *Why would women feel objectified?* In my culture in Hungary, just like in France, we feel admired and empowered by men. It's caused by the differences in our mindsets.

In the US (a masculine culture), where Emily's from, if a man looks at a woman in a sexual way, he's objectifying her. She becomes a sexual object. Hence, Emily is saying the advertisement is sexist. When a man objectifies a woman, he has the power.

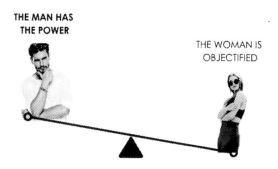

**THE MAN HAS
THE POWER**

THE WOMAN IS
OBJECTIFIED

**In masculine cultures, women feel objectified**

On the other hand, in France (a feminine culture) and many other cultures, including mine, if a man checks out a woman, he is empowering her. In these cultures, they believe that when a man looks at a woman in a sexual way, he isn't thinking clearly. Since he is distracted, he can't think straight; he can't think logically. Therefore, he has lost control; he has lost his power. As the woman can give what the man wants (sex), she can get anything she wants until she gives it to him. The woman has the power.

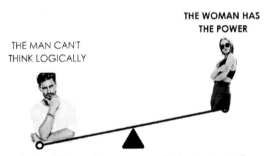

THE WOMAN HAS
THE POWER

THE MAN CAN'T
THINK LOGICALLY

**In feminine cultures, women feel empowered**

Perhaps Antoine's claim that "The woman has the power because she is beautiful, and she is naked" makes more sense now. The more a man wants a woman, the less he can think logically and the less power he has. On the contrary, he empowers her even more and makes her feel even sexier. Exactly as we discussed earlier, some cultures are masculine while others are feminine; we can see the same here. In masculine cultures, men have the power when it comes to them viewing women sexually, while in feminine cultures, women do.

You might ask, what happens when a man who is used to having the power starts dating a woman who is used to having the power? Could this be Katerina and Jack's problem? You might be onto something, but let's continue!

## Chivalry

Deep-rooted mindsets surround us everywhere we go.

In masculine countries in the West, where men have all the power (both authoritative as well as sexual), women often don't like men opening doors for them, pulling a chair out for them, or even helping them put their coats on. It makes women feel weak (and not equal) when they are perfectly capable of doing it on their own. On the other hand, in feminine cultures, where men empower women, chivalry (e.g., opening doors) is often appreciated. It makes women feel respected.

In Hungary, I grew up with this respect from men, and even though I think chivalry is unnecessary (as I am perfectly capable of doing things on my own), I highly appreciate it. Just like women do in Mexico - another feminine culture:

### MEXICO

*We like to look after women in general. For example, opening the car's door or picking up the check in a restaurant or – this one is quite rare but can happens – while walking on the sidewalk, men are always on the side nearest the road.*[xlviii]

This respect for women is not only shown through chivalrous gestures, but it is also often part of the language.

Greeting each other with a kiss on the cheek customarily evolved from hand-kissing – a gesture that was considered a respectful way to greet a lady. Traditionally, it was initiated by the woman, who offered her hand to a man to kiss. Today, hand-kissing is rare, but in several countries, the gesture is preserved in the language. For example, in Hungary, "Kezicsókolom" (I kiss your hand) or the more colloquial version "Kézcsók" (Hand kiss) is still often used.
Just like in Southern Italy, especially in the more traditional Sicily, where "Bacio le mani" (I kiss the hands) derived from its usage.[xlix]

A similar politeness and respect can be observed in many other areas. In feminine cultures, men respect and empower women, but women return this respect and empowerment, especially in private and at social events. The man is the head of the household, and they take the lead in family and social gatherings. It's a two-way street. Both men and women empower each other.

This is why many women who are from a feminine culture (just like Sylvie) often don't relate to feminism because, in these cultures, women already feel they have the power.

## summary

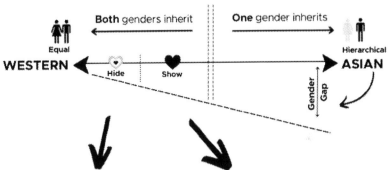

**Both** genders inherit → Equal · WESTERN · Hide · Show

**One** gender inherits → Hierarchical · ASIAN · Gender Gap

| ♡ **Masculine cultures** | ♥ **Feminine cultures** |
|---|---|
| • **Success & money-oriented** | • **People-oriented** |
| • Impress with their **achievements** | • Impress with their **personality and manners** |
| • **Men have the sexual power** | • **Women have the sexual power** |
| • **Women feel objectified** by the male gaze | • **Women feel empowered** by the male gaze |
| • Chivalry can make women feel **"weak"** or **"not capable"** | • Chivalry makes women feel **respected** |

## 8/2. THE MALE GAZE

You might be wondering, *is it, in fact, about women's mindsets, or is there something else?* Let's explore the root cause behind it: the male gaze.

Why does it make women feel objectified in one culture while empowered in another? Is there a difference between an objectifying and an empowering gaze?

To understand it, let's dive into masculine and feminine cultures a bit more. In feminine cultures, that show their feelings, people are usually comfortable with having eye contact, even with strangers, which can initiate emotions. From a very young age, people in these cultures grow up developing and trusting their own feelings - especially their sense of chemistry. Therefore, people in these cultures tend to flirt a lot. Flirting is a way to express that you like someone – it is a way to show your feelings.

In comparison, masculine cultures that hide their feelings flirt less openly and avoid revealing their feelings to each other too soon. Interestingly, these cultures are often not comfortable with looking deeply into someone's eyes, especially Western cultures that are very individualistic. It can even come across as invading someone's personal space. However, skipping this step and staring directly at a woman's body makes women feel objectified!

An empowering gaze starts with eye gazing and NOT the woman's body. This creates a personal connection and a kind of unspoken mutual agreement. It takes two to tango. You can't eye gaze unless both parties want to! So, the difference is that when you look into someone's eyes, it creates an opportunity for emotional connection. It builds trust and intimacy with the person. However, when you directly stare at someone's body, it is very one-sided and comes across as objectifying.

In the US and many other masculine cultures, men more frequently skip eye gazing because it can feel uncomfortable. Therefore, they look at a woman's body without her "consent," which leads to her feeling objectified.

On the other hand, in feminine cultures, looking at a woman's body without her consent reflects badly on the *man* as he has no manners. If you recall, feminine cultures impress each other with their personality and manners; hence, if a man skips eye gazing, it can easily ruin his chances!

So, let's talk about the elephant in the room. . .

How do you check out women RESPECTFULLY in feminine cultures? Having "permission" does not mean you can now go on a feast! Not at all! On the contrary. . .

You've got two seconds! That's about it.

One second down. . . and one second up.

Any more than that, and you risk becoming disrespectful – especially if you are not used to the game.

So, use your time wisely! ;)

However, that is not all. So, let's talk about the small print: the "Do's" and "Don'ts."

As we know, feminine cultures are focused on relationships. Therefore, personal connections are often about making the *other* person feel good rather than only caring about yourself. This is key, even when it comes to flirting!

So, as a man, do not:

Only fulfill your own needs by staring at the woman's body before looking away and continuing with your day. This is very one-sided and will just make the woman feel used!

Instead:

After you've got permission to check her out and get what you want, connect with her. Look her in the eye as a way to say, "Thank you" and acknowledge how pretty she looks! It can be purely by deep eye contact, or you can give her a half smile and barely visible nod before you go on your way. This might be a small thing, but it makes a huge difference!

This is why flirting is so common in feminine cultures; it makes both parties feel good. It's a win-win for both: men get to check women out, while women feel pretty and enjoy the attention. For this reason, in feminine cultures, it is not rare for women to initiate eye gazing! Purely because men make women feel beautiful.

Interestingly, an American woman who moved to Hungary several years ago mentioned in her YouTube video that one of the things she missed in Hungary was people complimenting her looks. Apparently, she got this a lot more in the USA.

I agree; we compliment each other a lot less verbally. However, if she were to read eye contact and body language, she would probably come to a very different conclusion.

Please note there is a big difference between eye contact and eye gazing! Eye contact is usually brief, and it usually doesn't count as a "mutual agreement," whereas eye gazing is longer and a lot deeper. It feels like you see someone's soul. They let you closer, and they let you in. It takes a lot of confidence, especially to do it with strangers. You don't get this feeling and level of intimacy with mere eye contact. This is usually the warm and fuzzy feeling that people who are not comfortable with eye gazing try to avoid. Eye gazing can help you to:

- recognize emotions,
- increase intimacy,
- build trust and connection.

I came across a YouTube video from Ollie, who talks about his feelings after running a seven-day eye gazing experiment with his girlfriend.[1]

Ollie – who sounds to be American – recently overcame some pretty severe anxiety. He felt he was disconnected from the people around him, as if there was a "mysterious three-inch glass" between them. Therefore, Ollie wanted to see if he could intentionally cultivate intimacy, depth, connection, and trust with those around him. This was when he decided to give eye gazing a try and run a seven-day eye gazing experiment with his girlfriend, Margarita. They both felt uncomfortable and guarded with it in the beginning, but became more and more comfortable with it over time.

According to Ollie, he began to experience feelings of love and acceptance, and honestly wanting the best for the other person. The more they practiced it, the more he found "love, trust, empathy, and connection really hard to resist" Ollie explains.

The goal of their experiment was to see if it genuinely increases connection, intimacy, and trust with someone. They both strongly agreed. Ollie said, "It's a wholehearted YES," while Margarita quoted a Portuguese expression:

"A gaze is worth more than a thousand words."

While watching the video, I found it interesting how Ollie called eye gazing a "practice." He would even put time aside to do it with his girlfriend. Or how Timothy Ferriss, the bestselling author of *The 4-Hour Workweek*, recommends learning eye gazing as one of his comfort challenges. They are both used to masculine cultures.

On the other hand, in feminine cultures – who show their feelings, eye gazing is a natural thing. People often do it even with strangers. It is a big part of flirting that is so deeply ingrained in feminine societies.

We can see the same pattern with PDA (Public Display of Affection). In feminine cultures that show their feelings, PDAs, e.g., kissing in the street, are okay. So much so that, in many of these countries, they don't even know what PDA means. Some don't even have a word or phrase for it! Just like we don't in Hungary. On the other hand, in masculine cultures that hide their feelings, PDAs are not normal and are often not accepted.

## summary

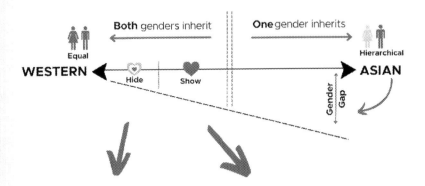

**Both** genders inherit      **One** gender inherits

Equal                      Hierarchical

**WESTERN**    Hide    Show            **ASIAN**

Gender Gap

|  Masculine cultures |  Feminine cultures |
|---|---|
| • **Hide** their feelings | • **Show** their feelings |
| • **Flirt less openly** | • Romantic & **flirt openly** |
| • Often **not comfortable having deep eye contact** - especially not with strangers. | • Often **comfortable with having deep eye contact** - even with strangers. |
| • Men more frequently **skip eye-gazing** and look directly at a woman's body, which makes women feel objectified. | • Men **start with eye-gazing** and not looking directly at the woman's body (which builds trust and makes women feel respected). |

## 8/3. HOW DO THEY PLAY "HARD TO GET"?

As we saw, Katerina and Jack were used to polar opposite power dynamics. But what about how their cultures play "hard to get"? Let's look at their differences and how it can lead to clashes.

Brace yourself! This is where it can get seriously tiring if you don't know the rules.

Women from feminine cultures might complain that men from masculine cultures are hard work. While men from masculine cultures often feel women from feminine cultures need a lot of "pampering." Or, women from masculine cultures might complain they never had to kiss a man first until they met one from a feminine culture.

It might feel like they have extremely different issues, but they come down to just two things: who has the power and what it is that they want?

Here comes the battle of the sexes. . . where men want physical intimacy while women seek emotional closeness.

**Battle of the sexes**

They play hard to get, to get what they want. But if it comes too easy, they won't appreciate it. If it comes too hard, it will put them off. So you can imagine what happens when our cultures play hard to get in polar opposite ways! Let's look at their dynamics.

*Masculine cultures:*

In masculine cultures (e.g., the USA), men have the power; therefore, they get what they want first: physical intimacy. In these cultures, sexual pleasure usually comes very early on in the dating phase. It is the start.

Men usually don't chase women until they get the physical intimacy they want. However, they start chasing afterward if they want more and want a relationship.

In these cultures, people usually hide their feelings to avoid being vulnerable. Therefore, they play "hard to get" by delaying emotional intimacy – which can often come across as playing mind/guessing games. This is what Jack was used to.

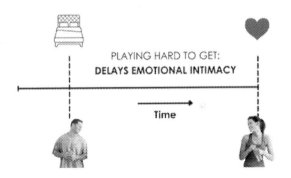

**Masculine cultures delay emotions**

On the other hand, for those who are used to a feminine culture, like Katerina, delaying emotional intimacy is impossible. This is because they are so used to showing emotions that they can't even imagine how you can start a relationship without it, let alone how it works.

For this reason, let me share with you a conversation I came across in a partially exaggerated video about American dating life. It perfectly reflects how masculine cultures play hard to get with emotions, so you can get a feel for it.

The video gives us a glimpse into the constant push and pull around emotional intimacy:[li]

We can see Michelle and Anna, who have been dating for a while, talking. However, as soon as Michelle reveals her feelings for Anna, Anna suddenly takes a step back.

Michelle, now concerned about getting hurt, decides to take a step back, too.

However, once Anna realizes this, she is suddenly back in, saying: "It definitely activates my self-worth issues, and I have to chase you to prove I am worthy of love."

However, Anna's move to chase Michelle activates Michelle's fear of commitment, and Michelle pulls back even more.

Anna concludes Michelle is emotionally unavailable and decides to back off for good, but as Michelle's fear has now subsided, Michelle is back in.

This is when Anna asks Michelle:
"Ok, so do you want a committed relationship?"

But Michelle leaves her hanging again, saying:
"Oh shit, I totally forgot! I have another date!"

This constant emotional limbo (playing hard to get with emotions) is the game of masculine cultures. When someone shares their feelings, the other feels vulnerable to getting hurt, so they instantly put their guard up.

To watch the full video, scan the QR code or visit our website:
howtodateaforeigner.com/resources

*Feminine cultures:*

On the other hand, in feminine cultures, women have the sexual power. Therefore, they get what they want first – emotional intimacy is the start. Women resist giving in sexually until the man is emotionally hooked. He then uses seductive language to get her to give in. They play hard to get by delaying sexual intimacy. This is what Katerina was used to.

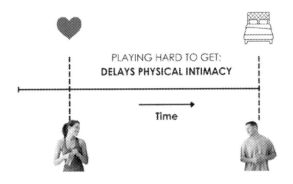

**Feminine cultures delay physical intimacy**

Here is where the twist comes: in these cultures, the more a woman likes a man, the longer she will make him wait for physical intimacy. This is to build an even stronger and deeper emotional bond, so once the man gets the physical intimacy he wants, he is already too invested emotionally to leave.

In masculine cultures where the male gaze makes women feel objectified, the word "seduction" has a very negative connotation to it. Therefore, in these cultures it is hard to imagine it as part of a positive skillset.

Yet, in feminine cultures, where women feel sexy and empowered by the male gaze, it is viewed as a very powerful tool and even an essential life skill. Feminine cultures are the masters of seduction.

Robert Greene describes it perfectly in his book, *The Art of Seduction*[iii]: "Thousands of years ago, power was mostly gained through physical violence. Nobody suffered more than women who had no weapon at their disposal, that could make a man do what they wanted. However, men had one weakness: their insatiable desire for sex.

"A woman could always toy with this desire, but once she gave in to sex, the man was back in control. If she withheld sex, he could simply look elsewhere. Women had no choice, but to submit to this condition. There were some though, whose hunger for power was too great. The greatest of them all was Cleopatra. Over the years these women found ways to turn this dynamic around. They invented seduction. With their appearance and showing only glimpses of flesh, they would tease a man's imagination. They would stimulate their desire not just for sex, but something greater: the chance to possess a fantasy figure. Once they had their victim's interest, they would get the man hooked and make him fall in love. Then women would turn cold and indifferent, confusing their victims. Just when the man wanted more, they found their pleasure withdrawn. They would be forced into pursuit to win her back and find themselves becoming the slave of the woman. The woman was no longer a sex object. She became a figure of power. However, in the 17th century, came a great change when men grew interested in seduction to overcome a woman's resistance to sex. They learnt to stimulate women's imagination and added a masculine element to the game: the seductive language. They discovered a woman's weakness for soft words. These two forms of seduction – the feminine use of appearance and the masculine use of language would often cross gender lines."

In feminine cultures like Katerina's, seduction is the game. Men love the hunt, and women enjoy the attention. You can see this in many Latin dances.

Chen Lizra, a professional dancer who has been traveling to Cuba for years, is fascinated by seduction. She explains in her Ted Talk[liii] that in Cuba, the dance of rumba is the game of seduction: the woman takes the role of the flirty hen, and the man is the seductive rooster.

"The woman uses her body to seduce the man, to say: '*Want it? Come and get it!*'"
The man will then use his body to demonstrate his masculinity and attempt to get her pregnant. The woman will notice the attack, block it, and mock him for not succeeding:

"'*Didn't make it. Try again!*'
Cubans interact every day as if they are playing the game of rumba. They keep a sexy tension always alive. It's like you could almost have it, but not. But if you only tried, then *maybe.*"

Even though seduction has been over-sexualized, it is more about knowing what you want and going for it, despite the number of rejections you encounter on the way - whether in dating or any other areas in life.

Seduction is about charm, self-confidence, pride and appeal. Strong self-confidence is crucial for seduction. Without it, you can't pursue what you want.

How Cubans integrate seduction and charm into their daily life can be seen across all feminine cultures in the West to a certain extent, from Eastern European countries to the temperamental Latin American ones.

Camille Chevalier-Karfis from Paris, who is the founder of French Today, explains how important the game is, even to French men:
"As for French men. Well, they are men. It's unlikely they'll refuse to take it further, but not unheard of. Again, the game is often more important than the catch, even to men."[liv]

While Marcelo tells us how confidence radiates from Brazilian women:

### BRAZIL

> *I've travelled a lot and I find Brazilian women to be one of the most confident in the world: how they dress, how they make love, how they act in a relationship, etc. It is very attractive. (Marcelo)*

Kerstin, on the other hand, who grew up in the Netherlands (masculine culture), sees Brazilian culture from a very different angle:

### BRAZIL vs. THE NETHERLANDS

> *I find South American men to be a lot more sexually driven and a lot more assertive. The men are very clear and open about wanting sex, and they see women as opportunities.*
>
> *Men in the Netherlands, where I grew up, are not like this. They are much more laid back and low-key. Although I think Brazilian men have gotten a lot better than they were in the past, they still have a long way to go to reach the equality that they have in northern Europe. (Kerstin)*

From *masculine cultures' perspective* like Kerstin's, it can seem like Brazilian men "see women as opportunities", so there is "a long way to go to reach equality", but in fact, it is the total opposite.

From a *feminine culture's perspective* (in Brazil, just like in France), desire is a sign of respect, and it empowers women. Hence women in these cultures often have very high self-confidence and self-esteem.

We often don't realize how different the games we play are:

Unlike in masculine cultures (like the Netherlands or the USA), where the chase starts after sexual intimacy (as men haven't got the emotional intimacy yet), in feminine cultures (like Brazil or Argentina), it is "game over." By that time, in feminine cultures, the man got everything he wanted (both emotions + sexual intimacy). There is no more challenge in it for him – unless the woman goes cold and makes him chase again.

Sarah, an Argentinian girl Aziz Ansari interviewed for his book titled *Modern Romance*, explains these dynamics. "When they are trying to pick you up, they really act like men. They will talk to you and talk to you until you hook up with them, and then they will act like girls. If you are not interested in them, they will become obsessed with you. If you are interested in them, they will disappear. It's like math. It's an equation."

Aziz Ansari explains Argentinians even have a word for it. "When it comes down to getting into a relationship, the Argentinians have a reputation for being hysterical. It's one of those culturally-specific words that is hard to define to someone who is not from the culture. It is someone who acts one way toward you initially and then completely reverses course. A woman who says 'no' 'no' 'no', and then finally 'yes' is said to be hysterical. As is a man who flirts madly then suddenly disappears for weeks without contacting you again."

This type of behavior is common in feminine cultures, not only in Argentina. However, the length of time a man would disappear after sex varies by country. The more temperamental a country is, the longer it can be. In the less temperamental Eastern European countries it might be just a few days or you might barely even notice it (especially, if you are used to the game). Whereas in Latin America it could be several weeks.

Based on what we know now, we can conclude that Katerina and Jack were used to very different dating games. Katerina was used to playing the game of seduction. She was used to getting emotions "on a plate" and making men work for sexual intimacy – which is how she always played hard to get.

However, Jack would not give Katerina the emotions until he got the sexual intimacy he was so used to starting with. Catch 22. . .

Knowing and recognizing these conflicting power dynamics can make a huge difference in your dating life.

*Seduction* (where emotional intimacy is the start) is the game of feminine cultures. Meanwhile *hookup culture* (where sexual intimacy comes first) is common in masculine cultures.

. . .but there is more!

However, let's do a quick summary first of what we have learnt in this chapter!

To watch Chen Lizra's TED Talk on seduction, scan the QR code or visit our website: howtodateaforeigner.com/resources

# summary

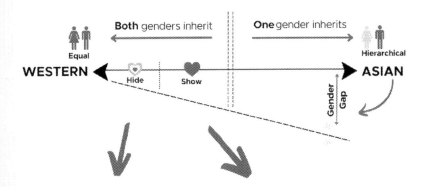

**Both** genders inherit — **One** gender inherits

Equal / WESTERN — Hide / Show — Gender Gap — Hierarchical / ASIAN

| 🤍 Masculine cultures | 🖤 Feminine cultures |
|---|---|
| • **Men** have the sexual power → **sexual intimacy is the start** | • **Women** have the sexual power → **emotional intimacy is the start** |
| • Play "hard to get" by **delaying emotional intimacy** | • Play "hard to get" by **delaying sexual intimacy** |
| • **Hookup culture is common** | • **Seduction is the game** |

## 8/4. WHAT IS THEIR DATING "DILEMMA"?

We all have a dilemma when we start dating someone:

*Do I want to give up my freedom for this person?*

We love our FREEDOM!

However, as masculine and feminine cultures have very different priorities, their approach is extremely different also!

| | Masculine cultures | Feminine cultures |
|---|---|---|
| Prioritize | Time (Tasks) | Relationships |

*Masculine Cultures*

Masculine cultures are focused on making money. Therefore, they are super organized with their time. They plan and keep to the plan. They have their (calendar) tasks queued up. However, they are not so decisive when it comes to relationships.

The Pimsleur Language Blog explains:

Americans are brought up knowing they have many options, and this also applies when it comes to choosing a romantic partner. As the saying goes: there is plenty of "fish in the sea." Hence, casual dating and having choices are commonly taken for granted. Settling down with one partner can be difficult when a "better" choice could be just around the corner.[lv]

**Choosing a partner in cultures who hide their feelings**

People in masculine cultures date *before* agreeing to be exclusive and starting a relationship. Therefore, Jack's dilemma is:

*Do I want to **GIVE UP** my freedom for Katerina?*

He is used to hiding his feelings and warms up slowly as he becomes comfortable with someone.

Partially for this reason, in masculine cultures, people often discuss with their friends whether someone is boyfriend or girlfriend material.

*Feminine Cultures*

On the other hand, feminine cultures like Katerina's are focused on relationships. They know their own feelings well and are very decisive when it comes to choosing a partner. However, as people in feminine cultures jump into a relationship a lot faster, they often have a backup plan in case it doesn't work out. They have a *queue* when it comes to their dating life, but often multitask when it comes to everything else.

It's as if you want the latest iPhone. If it comes out in two months' time, you are going to wait and work for it as that is your "Plan A." You are not going to buy a less desirable version. You want the iPhone. That's exactly how feminine cultures feel about relationships.

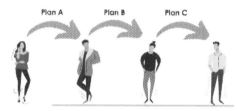

**Choosing a partner in cultures that show their feelings**

The queue is based on emotions. The person they like the most becomes "Plan A." However, if they meet someone new who they like even more, that person will "jump the queue" and become their new "Plan A" (and therefore their highest priority). The original "Plan A" loses their place in the queue and becomes "Plan B." It is not rare for people to have 3-5 people in their queue or even more; therefore, they are usually not single for too long. Hence when they are, it becomes a competition for the spot on their side.

Ryan explains:

### USA vs. ITALY

> *This makes me think of Italy, where dating is not a casual fling; instead, it is about your future. Dating someone is the first step in a committed relationship that hopefully leads to getting married and having children. This is why Italian girls can often appear competitive. They're trying to win that empty spot by your side. Culturally, it's a bit awkward to say you're dating several people when they view it as a significant experience and possibly the start of something lasting and meaningful. (Ryan)*

Feminine cultures assume exclusivity from the start. They date *after* being exclusive. Hence, they are "stuck" in limbo: they are exclusive but not in a relationship yet. So, they want to find out ASAP whether it is going to work or not. For this reason, Katerina's dilemma is:

*I put myself on hold for you. So, let's not waste each other's time and find out whether this is working ASAP! If not, let's break up so I can **GET BACK** my freedom and date someone else exclusively.*

Katerina is used to *showing her feelings and calms down slowly* as she becomes more comfortable with Jack.

So, in feminine cultures, it is always a race. A race to impress before the other person wants to cut their losses to get their freedom back. Just like in Brazil and Mexico:

### BRAZIL

> *If a man doesn't make a move rather fast, the woman will assume he's not interested and move on. Westerners can find it very confusing. (Emanuel)*

## MEXICO

> *In my experience, the dating rule for Mexicans is definitely one person at a time. The competition is real, and things move a lot faster than when following American dating norms. This doesn't just apply to Mexican women but also to men. (Santiago)*

People in feminine cultures don't usually seek their friends' advice. This is not only because they are a lot more in touch with their own feelings, but also because, due to their more hierarchical society, they need their parent's approval of their partner, not their friends.

In feminine cultures, people prioritize their relationships, and they multitask when it comes to everything else. Hence, they are often not the best at being on time. When it comes to dates, women are often late for dates too.

## BRAZIL

> *Try not to bother or be upset if she is late for a date. She was probably getting really pretty for you! So please compliment her, and don't complain.*[lvi]

### Similarly, in France. . .

Punctuality is not a thing, especially when it comes to dates. It is common to be "fashionably late." They even have an expression for it in France "le quart d'heure de politesse," which literally means "quarter of an hour of politeness." So, don't be offended if your French date is a few minutes late; it is not seen as disrespectful in France.[lvii]

On the other hand, if a man is late for a date, it is considered extremely disrespectful and almost unacceptable. The woman will highly likely not wait for him. So, let's summarize the two.

Do I want to **GIVE UP** my freedom for this person?

I put myself on hold for you. So, let's not waste each other's time and find out whether this is working ASAP! If not, let's break up, so I can **GET BACK** my freedom and date someone else exclusively.

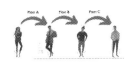

| Queue their priorities | 🤍 Masculine cultures | 🖤 Feminine cultures |
|---|---|---|
| **Queue** their priorities | **Tasks** | **Relationships** (queue their prospective dates) |
| **Multitask** in | **Relationships** (might date multiple ppl.) | **Tasks** |

**Decisive with their time,** but not so much with their relationships.

**Decisive with their relationships,** but not so good with their time.

## 8/5. HOW DOES IT AFFECT COMMUNICATION?

As our dating dilemmas can be so different, so is our communication. This is perfectly reflected in an article I came across in Psychology Today.[lviii] Let's start with this example first, then look at how Katerina's and Jack's situation was even worse.

According to the article, Olivia grew up in New Jersey, USA [masculine culture – who hides her feelings], while Antonio grew up in Brazil [feminine culture – who shows his feelings]. They met in the United States, after Antonio moved there for graduate school.

They have been dating for the last four weeks and Antonio really likes Olivia, but he is questioning whether she feels the same way about him. He began referring to her as his girlfriend about a week after they started going out. He doesn't want to date anybody else. But Olivia is not reciprocating it, calling Antonio her "boyfriend," and she seems indecisive.

For this reason, Antonio started questioning himself:
"I never questioned my dating experience in the past, but now I am thinking that my way of being with Olivia is abrasive or even aggressive."

In Brazil, Antonio and his friends never discuss whether someone is "girlfriend material" before they become exclusive with them. Therefore, Antonio became discouraged by Olivia even more.

Olivia on the other hand, explained that she likes Antonio very much, but she is questioning whether it is too soon. She feels she needs to slow down and consider why she is feeling the way she does before they start a relationship.

**"Dating Antonio feels like we are running 100 miles an hour."**

*Where do their problems come from?*

**Olivia (from the US)** is used to a masculine culture – where people date multiple people and need time to figure out their feelings. She is questioning whether she should give up her freedom.

**Antonio (from Brazil)** is used to a feminine culture – where people trust their own feelings. They compete for one person and assume exclusivity from the start. Antonio wants to figure out whether it is working ASAP or get his freedom back.

Now that we understand the differences between their approaches to dating, Olivia's and Antonio's situation starts making total sense:

Antonio (who is from a feminine culture – and trusts his own feelings) has put himself on hold for Olivia until they figure out whether it is working or not. He is in a race to impress her (talking and meeting frequently) before she changes her mind and moves on. However, in Olivia's eyes, his behavior comes across as too much. Olivia (from a masculine culture – who does not trust her own feelings as much) needs a lot longer time to figure out how she feels and whether she wants to date Antonio.

Those who are from a masculine culture, like Olivia, often perceive feminine cultures' behavior as needy.

On the other hand, Antonio finds Olivia *indecisive* and her behavior *discouraging*. Why? Because in Antonio's feminine culture, being forward means you are confident and decisive, which is super attractive to women in those cultures. You like the person, you know it, and you are not interested in anyone else (they are at the front of your queue; your "plan A"). However, to Antonio (who has put himself on hold for Olivia), it feels like Olivia is not trying. In his eyes, she is indecisive and *wasting his time*.

This is where dating cultures clash, and it is easy to see why: Decisive in one culture comes across as "needy" in the other.

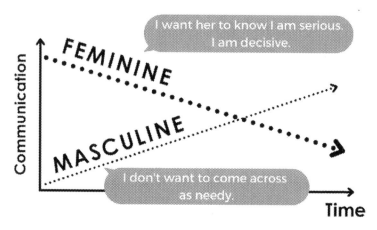

Masculine vs. feminine cultures' communication

Those who are from a feminine culture, like Antonio, often perceive masculine cultures' behavior as indecisive, discouraging, or wasting their time.

The problem? Unless Antonio is patient and they have amazing chemistry, he will cut his losses in a week or two, and by the time Olivia gets up to speed, he could be exclusive with somebody else.

Antonio could go on a date and be exclusive straight away. He might not need a long time to move on, especially if he has a queue of prospective dates.

## When Roles Reverse

If Olivia and Antonio's situation wasn't bad enough, for Katerina and Jack it got even worse.

In dating, there is a generally accepted principle: Men should chase women. Not the other way around.

Even though Olivia and Antonio had some issues, they didn't break this principle. As we recall, Antonio (the man) was used to the intense feminine culture, whereas Olivia (the woman), to the slowly warming up masculine one. So, in their situation, the man was chasing the woman.

However, the situation is even less fortunate for women who are used to the intense feminine culture, dating men from a masculine one. That's where things seriously start to fall apart!

This is because, unknowingly and unwantedly, the "roles" turn, and suddenly, it feels like the woman from the intense feminine culture is chasing the man from the slowly warming up masculine one. Nevertheless, it is highly likely that she won't even realize the issue until it is too late. Why? In feminine cultures, where women initially have the power when dating, they often feel empowered to initiate. On the contrary, in masculine cultures it is usually not normal. Therefore, it is a lot harder to rectify.

In fact, according to a reader on Quora's website:
"In America it is almost a hidden rule that girls do not hit on guys otherwise she is considered pathetic."[lix]

*Advice*

**If you are used to a feminine culture like Katerina's**, you will need to force yourself to take a step back and maybe even approach dating like a friendship until the other person is ready to call you their girlfriend or boyfriend. This will be extremely hard! However, if you go full-on, you will be way too intense for them and highly likely put them off.

**If you are used to a masculine culture like Jack's**, agreeing to date exclusively (even if you don't label each other) will give confidence to the person used to the feminine culture that you want it. You will come across as more decisive, and they will appreciate it. You can then take as long as you need to date – just make sure you communicate it.

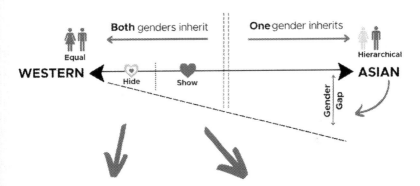

**Both** genders inherit — **One** gender inherits

Equal — Hierarchical

**WESTERN** — **ASIAN**

 Hide —  Show

Gender Gap

|  Masculine cultures |  Feminine cultures |
|---|---|
| • **Hide** their feelings<br>• **Warm up slowly**<br>• Being forward is perceived as: **desperate or needy** | • **Show** their feelings<br>• **Calm down slowly**<br>• Being forward is perceived as: **confident & decisive** (Finds the opposite: indecisive, discouraging and wasting their time) |

## 8/6. WHAT ABOUT DATING ETIQUETTE?

Many relationship experts give dating tips as if dating was universal. However, following American dating advice is a surefire way to ruin it if you are dating someone from Hungary. Therefore, it is important to take advice specifically by cultures. So, let's look at masculine and feminine cultures separately:

*Masculine Cultures*

Those from a masculine culture like Jack - where people hide their feelings, might take two months to date and meet around once a week. They message 1-2x a week in the beginning, and it gradually increases. They take their time. In these cultures, you should not message straight after the date, and the day after is also not recommended. You will come across as too needy, desperate to be in a relationship or inexperienced at dating and overly eager.

If you are from a feminine culture, especially if you are a woman, make sure to follow this rule, or you will give the wrong impression. In masculine cultures, if you message straight after a date, the man may think you just want to have sex. In these cultures, men should message first.

- **Three-Day Rule:**
  In an American TV series, *How I Met Your Mother*, the character Barney Stinson even popularized a three-day rule. A user on Urban Dictionary with the username RePent_22 explains it:

  The 'three-day rule' prevents a man from coming across as desperate or needy after getting a girl's phone number. According to this rule, you have to wait three days before contacting her to generate suspense and appear non-needy.[ix]

To watch the video clip from '*How I Met Your Mother*', scan the QR code or visit our website: howtodateaforeigner.com/resources

- **Three-Date Rule:**
  In masculine cultures (particularly in the USA), there is even a three-date rule. Jonathon Ashlay, a dating coach, explains that "some daters go by the third-date rule, a dating rule which dictates that both parties withhold sex until at least the third date."[lxi] - at which point a couple can have sex without being considered "too loose" to be a good partner.

  This is not a hard and fast timeline by which couples must have sex. Some in this culture will wait until date four or five or even longer.

*Feminine Cultures*

In feminine cultures, the rules are the polar opposite of masculine ones. This is because they show their feelings. Therefore, people in feminine cultures go through a very different emotional journey than people in masculine cultures do!

Let me explain. Imagine a person who explodes with anger. What happens? They can't control their emotions. They have an outburst. However, over time, they gradually calm down. This is the same emotional journey people in feminine cultures go through when they feel butterflies. They never learnt to hide their feelings. So, when they experience intense emotions, it is hard for them to keep them under control. This initial excitement is then reflected in their behavior: their speed and communication.

They don't have 2-3 months' time to waste on someone who is not going to work. They want to know it within weeks (they have people waiting in the queue). Hence the dating phase is much shorter, around 1-3 weeks, and a lot more intense.

They might even meet 3-4x a week and message several times a day (this is part of being very forward). To someone who is used to a masculine culture, this might feel like dating on steroids.

In these cultures, people usually reply within an hour (often within minutes). If they don't have time at all, then the latest by the end of the day (and in this case, they might even apologize for taking a long time to answer).

The longer they know each other, the less likely the other person will change their mind and want to "break up." They don't need to impress them anymore. Thus, the more comfortable they get with each other, the more relaxed they get with their communication.

You should message after the date (usually within hours, or at the latest, that night) that you had a good time. This is to let the other person know you are interested and want to see them again. It eliminates the guessing game and also shows you are confident and decisive. Brazilian women also expect men to call after a first date:

### BRAZIL

> *We really do not like 'mystery';*
> *we want the man to show interest [straight away].*[lxii]

Contrary to masculine cultures, in feminine cultures (especially in the less hierarchical ones), it usually doesn't matter who messages first. Partially because, in feminine cultures, the man takes the woman out on a date. He treats and cares for her and often pays on the first date – unlike in masculine cultures in the West, where they usually split the bill. So, after the date, in feminine cultures, women can message to say thank you, they had a good time and appreciated the great evening (this also helps to hold their place in the queue).

In feminine cultures like Katerina's, if someone doesn't message you for days, it doesn't mean they are playing it "cool." Instead, it means they are NOT interested, and you should get the hint! They are usually very forward (and intense) if they are interested. In these cultures, if you follow a three-day rule, you will most likely be labeled as a player!

France is a great example of a feminine culture. The Netflix series Emily in Paris also reveals the rules of text messaging in France:

Emily is trying to reach Alfie, the man from her French class. However, Alfie's phone keeps going to voicemail. She is about to re-record her last message to him when her French colleague, Julian, walks up to her. Emily, with hopelessness in her voice shares it with Julian how Alfie stopped replying to her texts. Then seeks

Julian's confirmation on whether that's bad. Julian explains: "Well, if it's been more than 24 hours, then he is not into you," and sarcastically adds: "Or, you should file a missing person's report!"[lxiii]

In feminine cultures like Katerina's, the rules of text messaging are just the tip of the iceberg when it comes to dating etiquette. If you recall, contrary to masculine cultures – where people impress with their achievements, in feminine cultures, they impress with their personality - a huge part of which comes down to manners. Therefore, if you are dating someone from a feminine culture, learning a bit of etiquette will go a long way! Let's look at two important ones for dates.

- **Picking a date location:**
  If you are a man, as tempting as it might be . . . picking the "best bar/restaurant" in town that *accidentally* happens to be right in your apartment block is not cool in feminine cultures.

  Instead: Start by asking which part of town your date is coming from. Either try to find a place to meet close to her or halfway between the two of you. Don't make her come to your doorstep (nor before nor after the date)! Instead, offer to pick her up/take her back home. She might decline your offer, but she will still appreciate it.

- **Ordering food/drinks:**
  You might be used to ordering yourself first, then let your date order theirs. However, if you want to follow the etiquette, this is the way:

  **Men:** ask your date up front what she would like to order.

When the waitress comes:

**Women:** Even if the waitress asks for your order, don't order. Instead, look at the man and let him order for you. Let him be a man!

**Men:** Show how attentive you are by still remembering her order. 😊

**Women:** If for any reason he messes up your order, communicate it to him, not the waitress! However, instead of saying, "That's not what I wanted!" just say, "Actually, could I get the … instead?" He will surely realize he messed it up but will appreciate you didn't embarrass him (and you might have just impressed him with your personality).

*Let's say your date was a success. . . what's next?*

Contrary to masculine cultures, where they usually meet only once a week and have a Three-Date Rule (to wait for at least three dates before physical intimacy), in intense feminine cultures, they might meet every day. In these cultures, having sex on the third date could mean only knowing someone for three days. Though there is a big difference among feminine cultures – some are a lot more liberal than others – having sex on the third date is usually considered way too fast.

In feminine cultures, women like to know someone a lot deeper before they have physical intimacy (if you recall, they need to hook the man emotionally). Even if they've known someone for only three weeks, it could mean they've had ten actual dates.

So, just because your date went well, don't rush things.

*Playing mind games*

Who is more into games: masculine or feminine cultures?
Place your bets, then let's find out!

## GERMANY

> *As a German man, I don't make a lot of moves. If you feel interested, tell me. I'm not into misinterpreting being nice with flirting.* (Michael)

## FRANCE

> *In general, I can agree they [French men] are more pushy, not always in a negative meaning. Personally, I liked the forwardness compared to Scandinavian men, who are more laid back. I hate the guessing game and enjoyed more straight and direct conversations.* (Brigitte)

## ITALY

> *They [men] will always approach you first; you will never be the one who tries to catch their attention.* [lxiv]

If we were to draw a conclusion purely based on this feedback, we could conclude:

Dating in masculine cultures (e.g., in Germany or Scandinavian countries) is often passive and full of guessing games as people are figuring out their feelings. On the contrary, feminine cultures (e.g., France or Italy) are very forward and hate guessing games.

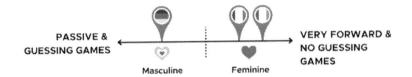

PASSIVE &
GUESSING GAMES

Masculine          Feminine

VERY FORWARD &
NO GUESSING
GAMES

However, the equation is not so straightforward because what we consider "games" and *when* we play games are different!

From Brigitte's French perspective, she is used to men being very forward before sex. Consequently, Scandinavian men (masculine culture) can come across as if they are playing games because they are not open with their feelings, especially in the beginning. They might contact her, then disappear for a few days before contacting her again. They play "hard to get" with emotions and play texting games (often not replying to messages for days).

However, if we asked a Scandinavian woman (masculine culture), she would complain of the exact opposite: French men play games *after* sex. Why? Because women in masculine cultures are used to men being forward after sex, exactly when French men would go cold. Interestingly, disappearing after sex is so expected in feminine cultures that it is often not considered as "playing games" (rather just "normal" and they know the person will return – just like how Sarah, the Argentinian girl, explained it in the chapter on Playing "Hard to Get"). However, it will drive someone from a masculine culture absolutely crazy.

On the contrary, playing the "three-day rule" (not messaging for three days) would come naturally for someone from a masculine culture, while it would drive someone like Brigitte (from a feminine culture) crazy, and she would consider it a game.

Hence, they both play games (whether they consider it a game or not)! So, when you tell someone, "I hate games!" and they agree...

but then continue doing the same behavior, they might not be lying! In their eyes, it might not be a game.

*Feminine cultures like Katerina's*, who communicate intensely in the beginning, will consider lack of communication before sex a "game" (as in this stage, people from feminine cultures would expect intense communication).

In contrast, *masculine cultures like Jack's*, who communicate more intensely after sex, will consider a lack of communication at that time a "game" (as in that stage, people from masculine cultures are used to frequent communication).

# summary

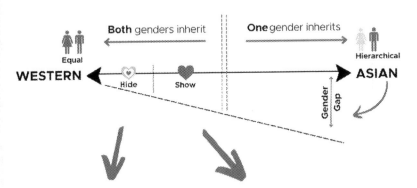

Both genders inherit → One gender inherits

Equal · WESTERN · Hide · Show · Gender Gap · Hierarchical · ASIAN

|  Masculine cultures |  Feminine cultures |
|---|---|
| • Dating is often passive & full of guessing games<br>• Communicate frequently after sexual intimacy | • Very forward & hate guessing games<br>• Communicate frequently before sexual intimacy |
| **Tips:**<br>• Do not message straight **after a date** or else you can come across as desperate or needy.<br>• If someone doesn't message you for days, they **might be playing it "cool."** | **Tips:**<br>• **Message straight after a date** to come across as confident and decisive.<br>• If someone doesn't message you for days, they are **NOT interested** |

## 8/7. WHY DO YOU FEEL REJECTED (WHEN YOU'RE NOT)?

Da Nang, Vietnam, May 2020

I was getting ready to go to sleep when I heard my phone beep. It was a message from Kira, a Ukrainian girl I had gotten to know a few weeks earlier. Even though we had barely just met, we became friends very fast. With her energy, kind personality, and contagious smile, it would have been hard not to be friends with her. She was a real people magnet, full of confidence and laughter.

Two weeks prior, she met a guy from New Zealand – the tall, dark, handsome type. They clearly had chemistry, even though Kira tried her best not to admit it. "He is just a friend," she said, but soon after, they had their first date. It was going all too well. Kira was on cloud nine.

However, slowly she started becoming anxious.

"Do you think I should text him?" she asked. "I haven't heard from him since this morning." . . . Kira was from a feminine culture.

Just as I was to reply, she sent me one of those never-ending text messages you can just scroll and scroll without an end in sight.

"Shall I send this?" she asked.

"No, Kira, you are ruining it! Just wait for him to reply. Go to sleep!"

It took some time to convince her, but eventually, she agreed. . . "OK."

Fifteen minutes later, my phone beeped again.

"How about this? I made it shorter."

It started getting frustrating, but I knew exactly what she was going through.

A few weeks later, Kira reached out to me for help. "I don't know what to do. I just keep waiting for his messages. I have classes to teach, but I barely get any sleep at night. I can't work, I can't train, I don't have any appetite, and I'm exhausted."

Let's look at what happened to Kira. Why did she turn from someone super confident and full of life into a totally different person within just a couple of weeks? Could it be that something very similar has happened to Katerina? If yes, why? And how can you avoid it happening to you?

As we are now aware, feminine cultures communicate frequently in the beginning, while masculine cultures start infrequently and warm up slowly.

As John Bowlby, a British psychologist and the first attachment theorist, discovered, one of the conditions that can trigger anxiety is being rejected by others, such as a relationship partner.

One of the ways we often conclude someone is rejecting us is based on their frequency of communication.

- If they contact us frequently > they like us
- If they barely talk to us or even ghost us > they reject us

We can feel rejected in any culture; however, there is an even higher probability when it comes to cross-cultural dating – purely because our expectations for frequency of communication are different.

It is the same feeling when you are used to getting lots of likes on social media, and suddenly overnight, your posts are not getting any. Instead of blaming the algorithm, you start questioning why people don't like it. What are you doing wrong?

This sense of rejection can trigger each party at various stages to become anxious, insecure, and obsessed with their partner, which they will have an extremely hard time letting go of.

In this chapter, we will explore when we are likely to misunderstand someone's frequency of communication as a rejection and at what stages we need to be careful to ensure we don't end up in Kira's shoes.

Let's look at the two stages where we can misunderstand communication frequency: before and after sexual intimacy.

### Before sexual intimacy

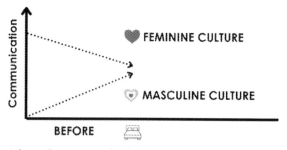

**Misreading communication frequency before sexual intimacy**

Someone who is used to a feminine culture like Kira and Katerina is used to communicating frequently in the beginning. This frequent communication reassures them that the other person feels the same way. However, if they date someone from a masculine culture, who is used to infrequent communication, this lack of communication will make the person from the feminine culture feel rejected. Why? Because we often "translate" infrequent communication as we are *not liked* or that we are *being rejected*.

This is exactly what happened to Kira and Katerina. Kira grew up in a feminine culture, and she could always trust her feelings. However, for the first time, she felt as if she could not. She felt there was a strong chemistry between them, but his lack of communication made her feel rejected. She started questioning herself.

Therefore, someone who is used to frequent communication in the beginning can feel "rejected" by the masculine culture's infrequent approach.

This is precisely how Katerina felt with Jack when she hadn't heard from him for days after they said goodbye. She was really confused because there was a strong chemistry between them. However, Jack gave the opposite signals with his communication. Katerina was used to men being very forward and communicative when they are interested, but Jack was not. The more Katerina reached out to Jack, the more rejected she felt when she didn't hear back.

This sense of rejection will be enough to trigger the person to become anxious. They will end up in a cycle that is extremely difficult to get out of.

Let's look at it step-by-step how it plays out in real life between a feminine and masculine culture.

## Anxious attachment:

The diagram below shows the sequence of events that can trigger the more frequently communicating partner to become anxious. Let's look at it in relation to the case of Katerina and Jack. Katerina is from an initially frequently communicating feminine culture and Jack is from a slowly warming up masculine one:

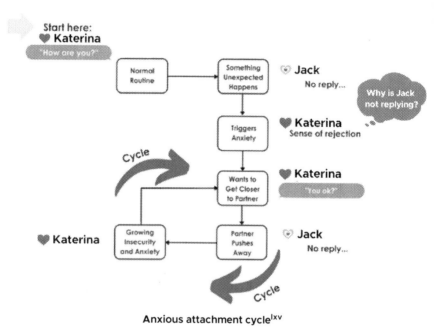

Anxious attachment cycle[lxv]

Infrequent communication from Jack provokes anxiety in Katerina, who then tries to reduce it by seeking closeness to Jack. However, when Jack rejects this request for greater intimacy it increases Katerina's insecurity and anxiety even more. Hence Katerina gets locked into a cycle with Jack: the frequently communicating Katerina tries to get closer, but the infrequently communicating Jack rejects the request for greater closeness. This leads the frequently communicating Katerina to try even harder to get closer, followed by another rejection from Jack, and so on.[lxvi]

Danielle, the author of *The Love List* blog explains how it feels:

When someone you're dating starts acting slightly differently, you jump to the conclusion they don't want to be with you anymore. You get so badly affected by your fear of rejection that it's all you can focus on. However, instead of driving that person away, you attempt to draw them closer. You cling on, like your life depended on it, because you can't bear the thought of them leaving. When, in fact, they might just need a little space, which is totally fine.[lxvii]

The outcome? The person from the feminine culture becomes obsessed with the masculine partner and explodes their inbox.

The person from the feminine culture will seek closeness. They are used to positive affirmations (and frequent communication from their partner). However, the masculine partner's infrequent communication makes the partner from the feminine culture insecure, who then seeks even greater closeness and reaches out again, hoping for a reply. The person from the feminine culture then ends up in a never-ending cycle of seeking closeness.

All this, while the avoidant masculine partner's only wish is in the words of Danielle: "Please don't crowd my space."

The person from the feminine culture is suffocating the masculine one. Meanwhile the masculine partner is triggering the person from the feminine culture to become increasingly anxious.

Exactly like Kira, Katerina, and Antonio from Brazil, who showed signs of becoming anxious, questioning his way of being with Olivia, I became anxious myself (feminine culture) within just two weeks of meeting the American guy (masculine culture). It then took me two years just to figure out what was happening to me and another year to feel fully secure again. All this, purely due to our communication differences between cultures!

Suzanne Collins, in her novel, The Hunger Games: Mockingjay, says, "It takes ten times as long to put yourself back together as it does to fall apart." I could not agree with it more!

It can be a crazy long process – both being trapped in the cycle as well as recovering from it. Most people I've met who experienced it couldn't get out of the cycle for several years. Therefore, it is important to know how different dating styles behave and how they can affect you, so you can prepare yourself and approach the situation with an informed perspective.

You might be wondering: *How come I became anxious this time and not with my American ex? Didn't we have the same communication issues back then?*

In fact, we did. However, there was one thing that made a massive difference. Very early on in our dating, when we would usually be communicating a lot in feminine cultures, he told me one sentence that turned everything around. This sentence was:

"You don't let me miss you!"

I was so shocked, I still recall thinking:

*Fine, suit yourself! You can message me when you "miss me."*

However, in hindsight, it prevented me from becoming anxious. From that day onward, I moved him to the back of my queue.

I was extremely annoyed and for around a month or two I only replied to messages. I *never* sent a text first.

We didn't know anything about our cultural differences, but purely him communicating his problem, helped us resolve it. It gave him time to warm up while at the same time, I calmed down.

*After sexual intimacy*

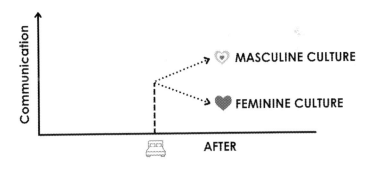

Misreading communication frequency after sexual intimacy

After sexual intimacy, the tables turn.

By now, Jack from the masculine culture has warmed up to Katerina and, in his culture, if men want a relationship, they start chasing after sex. On the other hand, Katerina from the feminine culture has calmed down and does not feel the constant need to try to impress Jack. Plus, in her culture, they go cold after sex.

Therefore, Jack from the masculine culture becomes the more frequent communicator from the two of them, risking him becoming anxious. So, how does it play out?

Jack from the masculine culture was used to Katerina's intense communication in the beginning, but now he is not getting it.

He starts wondering whether there is a problem. Even though Katerina from the feminine culture says, "Everything is okay," Jack keeps questioning whether it is. This lack of communication from Katerina then triggers Jack to become anxious, insecure, and obsessed with Katerina. They end up in the exact same cycle that Katerina from the feminine culture got trapped in prior to sexual intimacy.

This is how cultural differences in dating can make us feel rejected when in reality, the other person might actually be interested. Someone with a confident and secure personality can become extremely insecure in as little as a few weeks!

In both scenarios (before or after sexual intimacy – irrelevant of the person's communication style and whether their culture is masculine or feminine), the cycle only ends when:

- **the infrequently communicating partner** finally responds and validates their partner's need for closeness.

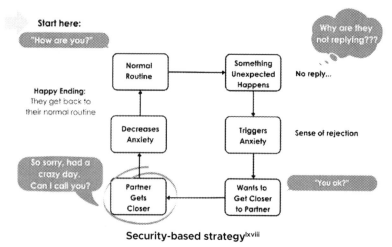

**Security-based strategy**[lxviii]

- **the frequently communicating partner** gives up getting a response, and the relationship effectively dies.

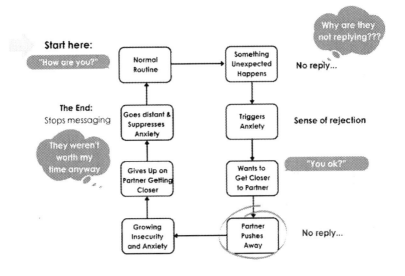

**Attachment avoidant strategy**[lxix]

*Advice for people from:*

**Feminine cultures like Katerina's:** If you are dating someone from a masculine culture, you have the highest chance of becoming anxious before sexual intimacy. Therefore, you need to practice a lot of self-control and cut back on communication at this stage. The moment you feel you want to message a second time before getting a response is the first sign you are getting anxious!

Instead, take a step back and give them time to miss you. Go for a long walk or turn your phone off if you really have to! The key is to wait for them to reply.

**Masculine cultures like Jack's:** If you are dating someone from a feminine culture, you need to be especially careful after sexual intimacy. It's hard to specify the time frame, but the first week or two will be the most difficult. As hard as it will be, this is when you need to play it "cool." If you don't, the experience could result in long-lasting anxiety for you – similar to what can happen to people from feminine cultures. You won't be able to move on!

Therefore, treat them like you would treat someone in the early stages of dating in your own culture. Give them a bit more space.

So, let's summarize the differences between the two.

# summary

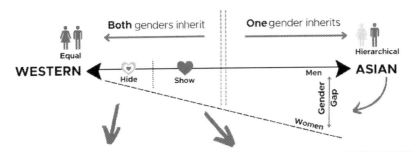

**Both** genders inherit

**One** gender inherits

Equal
**WESTERN**

Hierarchical
**ASIAN**

Hide

Show

Men

Gender Gap

Women

|  Masculine cultures |  Feminine cultures |
|---|---|
| **BEFORE sexual intimacy:** <br><br> • Communicate **infrequently** (warm up slowly). | **BEFORE sexual intimacy:** <br><br> • Communicate **frequently** (calm down slowly). <br> • **Chase before sexual intimacy** (seduction is the game). <br> • **RISK OF BECOMING ANXIOUS & FEELING REJECTED** before sexual intimacy due to masculine culture's infrequent communication at this stage. |
| **AFTER sexual intimacy:** <br><br> • **Chase after sexual intimacy.** <br> • Communicate **frequently** (warmed up and feel comfortable). <br> • **RISK OF BECOMING ANXIOUS & FEELING REJECTED** after sexual intimacy due to feminine culture's more relaxed communication (or disappearance) at this stage. | **AFTER sexual intimacy:** <br><br> • **Go cold after sexual intimacy.** <br> • Communicate **less frequently** (calmed down and feel comfortable). |

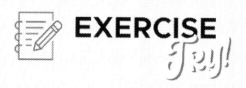

## KATERINA AND JACK ON A DATE

Now that we are familiar with how different Katerina's and Jack's mindsets are, let's put the pieces of the puzzle together. We're going to look at how cultural differences in dating can trigger a chain reaction – often without us even realizing it.

Try to help Katerina from Bulgaria (feminine culture), figure out what went wrong on her date with Jack from Vancouver, Canada (masculine culture). There are several guiding questions to help you.

To get the most out of it, focus on:

- Things that might feel *strange or different* to them
- Things that might bring out *negative feelings* in them (and why?)
- How they would react

The second half of this chapter will then reveal the exact thoughts and feelings Katerina was going through at each stage.

**Katerina explains:**

"Very early into our date, Jack started telling me about his career and education, which turned into a half-an-hour-long conversation.

However, in my culture, we don't talk about these areas as much during the early parts of dating – especially not on a first date. Our dates are more about finding common interests and having fun."

**What is the difference between how Jack tried to impress Katerina and what Katerina was used to in her culture?**

Jack tried to impress Katerina with:

Katerina was used to people impressing with:

**How do you think Jack's approach made Katerina feel?**

**Why could it be a problem?**

**Katerina continues:**

"We had a really nice date, but then Jack asked me if I wanted to go over to his place. It felt so disrespectful. Why ruin it like that?"

**Given that Katerina is from a feminine culture, what could have Jack misinterpreted as a sign that he can make a move?**

**How could his move have affected their power dynamics?**

**Katerina:**

"After we said goodbye, he disappeared from the face of the earth. I hadn't heard from him for days – even though he clearly seemed interested. In my culture when men are interested, they are very forward and communicative, but Jack really confused me."

**If Jack liked Katerina, why didn't he contact her?**

**How do you think Katerina interpreted Jack's silence?**

**Katerina:**

"I liked him, but because he didn't chase me, I started questioning whether I had impressed him enough. I started to feel I had to prove myself."

**What beliefs could have made Katerina feel she needed to try to prove herself?**

**What did Katerina believe that proving herself would change?**

**In reality, would it have changed Jack's behavior? Why? Why not?**

**Katerina:**

"The more I reached out to him, the more rejected I felt."

**Why did Katerina feel rejected?**

**How is communication different in Katerina's and Jack's cultures?**

**If Jack liked Katerina, how could he have changed the situation?**

**What should Jack learn from his date with Katerina? What should he do differently next time if he is dating someone from a feminine culture?**

**What should Katerina learn from her date with Jack? What should she do differently next time if she is dating someone from a masculine culture?**

# SOLUTION

## WHAT WENT WRONG?

Katerina's first culture shock was how much information Jack shared about his career and education. Even though talking about these on a first date wasn't "taboo" in her culture, she still wasn't used to discussing them for half an hour. She was more used to finding common interests and having fun.

This is due to differences between Katerina's and Jack's cultures:

In success- and money-oriented cultures like Canada, people try to *impress with their achievements* (job, money, education).
In these cultures, "résumé exchange," discussing someone's education and career is a big part of first dates.

On the contrary, lifestyle- and people-oriented cultures like Katerina's, try to *impress with their personality and manners.*

You might think: *Ok, we are all different. Why is that a problem?*

Trying to impress with your achievements can hinder power dynamics. This was exactly what happened to Katerina and Jack.

In Katerina's feminine culture, *initially*, women have the power (until the woman gives up her power - when she has sex with the man).

Therefore, in the early stages, Katerina (in her culture) was used to power dynamics that look like this:

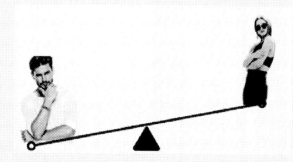

In feminine cultures like Katerina's, women are used to being admired, empowered, and respected by men.

*Katerina shares her thoughts and feelings:*

"When Jack tried to impress me with his achievements, he pulled the rug from under my feet. Instead of making me feel admired and respected in the initial stage, which I was so used to, Jack's achievements started messing with my head. I started questioning:

'Are my achievements enough (for Jack to respect me)?'

I needed some kind of validation, but I was not getting it. Instead, I got the polar opposite: Jack asking me to go over to his place.

With this question, however, Jack totally ruined it for me. I was used to having the power on my side – which also meant having respect. However, Jack's question screamed: 'No respect.'"

Purely by inviting Katerina to his place, Jack flipped the scale to his side. Now he had the power, which messed up the power dynamics for Katerina.

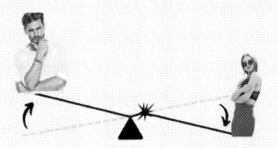

This often happens, when men from masculine cultures, where people hide their feelings, go on a date with a woman from a culture where they show them.

Camille Chevalier-Karfis, who was born and raised in Paris, explains: "You will know when a French girl is flirting with you: she'll smile to excess, move her hair a lot, smile at you, blush, laugh hard and loud at your jokes, find occasions to touch your shoulder (or even your knee... ooh la la),... and it's not unlikely that she'll make the first move. So relax and enjoy the show :-)"[lxx]

However, men from masculine cultures, where they are not used to so openly showing their feelings, often misread this flirty behavior as 'She is up for it' and think they can make a move (inviting the woman over to their place).

The irony is though that they are actually ruining their own chances. *Why?* Because in feminine cultures like Katerina's, where men empower women, many women have very high self-esteem, and they would never sleep with a man who does not treat them with respect. However, inviting a woman over to a man's place (especially on the first few dates) is extremely disrespectful in feminine cultures and makes women feel objectified.

*Katerina continues:*

"When everything that has always worked in my culture started failing me, I had one last hope for validation – if Jack chased me. However, I kept getting polar opposite signals than I was used to: Jack was not chasing me."

In Katerina's culture, just like in many Latin American countries, men chase before sex (this is what Katerina was used to). However, in Jack's culture, in Canada, men chase after. So now, Katerina was not only questioning whether her achievements were "good enough," and whether Jack respected her, but as Jack did not chase her, she started to feel she had to prove herself.

. . . Suddenly, Katerina was up against an impossible task: to flip the scale back onto her side – to get her power back.

*Katerina explains:*

"Without consciously realizing it, I started to compete for something I had never had to compete for before – a man's respect.

Which is far from healthy, as men in my culture want someone who supports them and not who competes with them."

Things started escalating further. . . The more Katerina reached out to Jack, the more rejected she started to feel. This was because even their cultures' approach to communication was the polar opposite.

Katerina was used to communicating frequently with someone in the beginning and calming down slowly the more comfortable she got. However, in masculine cultures like Canada, initially they communicate infrequently and warm up gradually. Therefore, as Jack did not reciprocate Katerina's frequent communication, every time she reached out, she felt more and more rejected.

*Katerina shares how she felt:*

"When dating has always 'worked' for you, but suddenly nothing works, and you do not understand why, you start overthinking everything, such as, *If I send a message, what will he reply?*

I ended up constantly trying to be a step ahead of Jack.
It became extremely tiring and draining. I became so fixated on the problem of why nothing is working that was *supposed* to be working, that I couldn't sleep or focus. I lost my creativity, and even sense of humor. Within just weeks, I went from being on top of the world confident to super anxious and insecure. Purely due to cultural differences in dating!"

DATING STYLE

Different mentalities in our societies formed differences in our behavior. They are reflected in our daily interactions. One of the most visible manifestations of this is the way we greet each other:

- **Hugging:** There are countries where people hug each other when they meet. This is common in masculine cultures (e.g., the USA) where men and women are close to equal in society, but they hide their feelings.
- **Kissing:** In other countries, it is common for people to greet each other with a kiss on the cheek. It is typical in feminine cultures (e.g., Brazil) where they show their feelings.
- **Bowing:** In countries where they bow (e.g., Japan), the greeting style reflects the hierarchy in their society.

Greeting styles reflect not only a culture's mentality but also its dating style. Therefore, we are going to use them to distinguish between the four distinctively different dating styles.

When we look at them on the cultureZ™ spectrum, this is how our greeting styles reflect the mentalities of our societies:

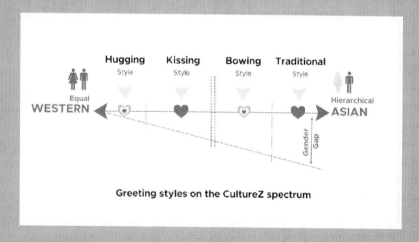

**Greeting styles on the CultureZ spectrum**

Let's now explore the four dating styles.

# CHAPTER 9

#  HUGGING STYLE

## COUNTRIES WHERE IT IS COMMON

The Hugging Style is typical in countries, where historically, Protestantism spread as the main religion, even if it is not widely practiced today. Mostly, this was in Anglo-Saxon, Germanic, and Scandinavian countries, such as the USA, UK, Canada, Australia, New Zealand, Germany, Denmark, or Sweden, as shown on the map below.

**Countries with the Hugging Style**

**WHAT ARE THEIR MINDSETS & BELIEFS?**

Everything we have learnt about *masculine cultures* reflects the mindset of the Hugging Style. Let's review what they were:

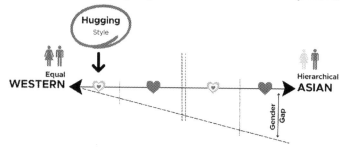

- **Men and women are close to equal in society**
    - They date to find love
    - They usually split the bill
    - They often dress casually for dates
    - Introducing the parents is not a big step
    - Seeking friends' approval is important

- **Society is success- and money-oriented (masculine); they hide their feelings**
    - Men have the power
    - They start with physical intimacy (hookup culture)
    - They play hard to get by delaying emotions
    - They impress with their achievements
    - They might date multiple people at the same time
    - They often date for two months or even longer (debating whether to give up their freedom)
    - Communication: warms up slowly (three-day rule)

## WHAT ARE THEIR DATING STAGES?

The Hugging Style is the most clearly structured out of the four styles. The phases of the relationship are distinctly defined. So, you are taking small steps to figure out whether the relationship works for you.

In the image, you can see that the Hugging Style is very structured.

It consists of *phases* (e.g., dating) and *milestones* ( **1-1** , Ö ).

In the Hugging Style, the emphasis is on the milestones.

- **Dating** (phase)
- **Exclusivity talk** **1-1** (milestone)
- **Relationship** (phase)
- **Engagement** Ö (milestone)
- **Preparing for marriage/Engaged** (phase)

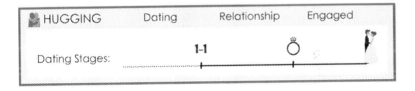

Dating stages of the Hugging Style

As these stages can be different from one dating style to the next, let's look at them in more detail in the Hugging Style.

- **Dating phase**: This is when you are trying to figure out whether you like the person. In the Hugging Style, people often try to figure out their feelings at this stage.
  - o Date multiple people because they are not (yet) exclusive when in the dating phase.
    (Indicated by the dotted line, while an exclusive relationship is a solid line.)

- ○ Have physical intimacy (even though they are not in a relationship).

- **Exclusivity talk ( 1-1 )**: It's an "official" verbal agreement to become a couple and start a relationship.
  Properly timing the exclusivity talk is important. You don't want to do it too early, when the other person is not ready, as it can be awkward, or you could scare them off. Yet if you leave it too late, your partner might go exclusive with someone else.
  - ○ The exclusivity talk is usually initiated by the man and is often called "the talk."

- **Relationship phase**: This is a period of more committed and intentional dating where the couple assess whether they are the right fit for each other in order to eventually get married.

- **Engagement ( O )**: The man kneels down in front of the woman and asks her to marry him. In these cultures, there is a lot of emphasis on the ring, which should be big.
  In the USA, for example, men, on average, spend three months of their salary just on the ring.

- **Preparing for marriage (Engaged):** It is often an odd period where most couples feel as if they are married at the point a proposal is accepted. They are just waiting for the wedding to happen, so that it can be official. It is like they are in a "no man's land" where they are just waiting to be married. This is because, in the Hugging Style, milestones like "the talk," "proposal," and "wedding" are the highlights, as opposed to the periods of time between them.

## When do they become official?

One of the big differences among dating styles is at *what stage* you become official. In other words, at what stage do you consider each other as girlfriend and boyfriend? This is partially what Olivia and Antonio struggled with (if you recall their story from the chapter titled "How does it affect communication?"). Olivia was used to the Hugging Style.

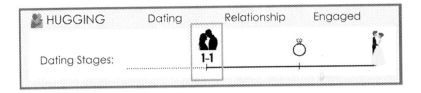

**Becoming official in the Hugging Style**

**Becoming official :** In the Hugging Style, you become official at the same time as the exclusivity talk **1-1**. Therefore, once you have agreed to be exclusive, you will consider your partner as your girlfriend or boyfriend.

## *How long do they wait to say, "I love you"?*

Another interesting difference among cultures is how long people wait to say, "I love you." Of course, it can vary a lot depending on chemistry and your unique circumstances, but the differences are clearly noticeable.

Several American users on the forum Reddit agreed it takes a pretty long time. Approximately between six months to a year once the couple has been exclusive. The Brits also tend to wait around six months, according to an article on Body+Soul.[lxxi]

One user expressed that "the English phrase 'I love you' in a romantic context is a very heavy sentence to hear." He explained: "Saying 'I love you' is the signal that we want the relationship to be even more serious, we see a potential future with the other person, we are fully committed to them. As other posters [on the forum] have said, six months to one year after becoming exclusive is a normal time frame to say or hear it. Of course, everything I am saying is GENERALIZATIONS, and there are couples who become committed very quickly, too. But *generally*, most would find it 'clingy' or 'desperate' to hear 'I love you' from their boyfriend/girlfriend very quickly."[lxxii]

Now let's look at the Kissing Style, to understand Olivia and Antonio's problem.

**The Hugging Style** is common in Anglo-Saxon, Germanic, and Scandinavian countries.

**Mindset:**

Men and women are close to equal in society, they hide their feelings.

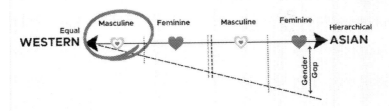

Equal — Masculine — Feminine — Masculine — Feminine — Hierarchical
**WESTERN** ← ... → **ASIAN**
Gender Gap

**Dating Stages:**  Dating  Relationship  Engaged

Dating Stages:  1-1

**Assumptions:**  NO ASSUMPTIONS

# CHAPTER 10

# 😙 KISSING STYLE

## COUNTRIES WHERE IT IS COMMON

The feminine Kissing Style is common where Catholicism, Orthodoxy, and Judaism were historically the main religions – independent of how widely they are practiced today. Mostly, this was in Eastern European, Mediterranean, Latin American, and many Sub-Saharan African countries (e.g., Hungary, Russia, France, Italy, Spain, Brazil, Cuba, Cameroon, or even Israel), as shown on the map below.

**Countries with the Kissing Style**

Please note that the Kissing Style spreads across a much wider variety of countries than the other styles. It goes from Eastern European, Mediterranean, and most Latin American countries (where both son and daughter inherit equally) to the more conservative and very hierarchical African countries (where properties and status are commonly passed from fathers to sons only). Hence, the Kissing Style has both types: where both genders inherit or where only one does.

Many people who are used to Asian dating cultures often associate "Western dating" with the *masculine* Hugging Style. Thanks to Hollywood movies, "Western dating" became the synonym of American dating culture. However, the *feminine* Kissing Style couldn't be more different, so it's important to understand them both.

## 👀 WHAT ARE THEIR MINDSETS & BELIEFS?

Everything we have learned about *feminine cultures* reflects the mindset of the Kissing Style. Let's review what they were:

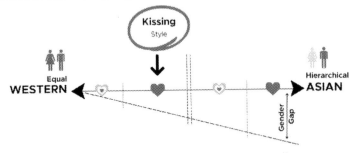

- **Men and women are close to equal in society (it is slightly hierarchical)**
  - ○ They date to find love
  - ○ Often, men pay on dates
  - ○ They usually dress smart casual for dates
  - ○ Introducing the parents is a key step
  - ○ Getting their parents' approval is important

- **Society is people and lifestyle-oriented (feminine); they show their feelings**
  - ○ Women have the power (initially in dating)
  - ○ They start with emotional intimacy (seduction)
  - ○ They play hard to get by delaying sexual intimacy
  - ○ They impress their date with their personality
  - ○ They compete for one person
  - ○ They skip the dating phase (fast-track to a relationship)
  - ○ Communication: calms down slowly (reply instantly)

## 👄 WHAT ARE THEIR DATING STAGES?

Having grown up in Brazil, Antonio was used to the Kissing Style. The Kissing Style can be hard for others to understand because of the lack of structure. Actually, there is a structure, but it's well-hidden beneath the surface, which is close to impossible to recognize if you didn't grow up in it. Even though I did, it took me years to define its stages. I kept missing many small but crucial details to be able to understand the Kissing Style fully myself. This is because certain stages blend into each other within it, but there are clues to help you know when you've reached that stage.

Let's look at its stages:

You will see that the Kissing Style is the least structured. It's more about going with the flow. Contrary to the Hugging Style, in the Kissing Style, people often embrace the *process* (e.g., dating), not the milestones (⌾). There are the following stages:

- **Dating/Relationship** (phase)
- **Engagement** ⌾ (milestone)
- **Preparing for marriage/Engaged** (phase)

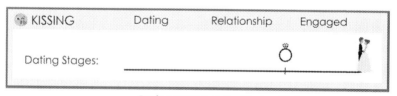

Dating stages of the Kissing Style

Let's look at them in detail:

- **Dating phase/Relationship**: One of the biggest shocks about the Kissing Style for people who are used to the other styles is that they date *after* being exclusive, not before.

  For this reason, you will notice that the exclusivity talk is missing. Especially those who are used to the Hugging Style find it extremely fast and confusing. How can we know so soon that we want to be in a relationship with someone we've just met? Let me spoil it now: we don't! We just know we really like the person and would like to give it a chance.

  Often, the dating phase starts with the first kiss (or is naturally assumed after a few dates) and then gradually progresses into a relationship without an exclusivity talk (because you were already exclusive from the start). Due to the assumed exclusivity and the gradual progression into a relationship, it is often hard to tell when the dating phase was. However, we will come back to this in a bit, and it will start making sense!

- **Engagement (⌾):** The proposal is often the first real milestone in the relationship. However, contrary to the Hugging Style, in the Kissing Style, there is a lot less emphasis on the ring. The ring is usually a lot more modest as the proposal is more about the feelings than the event itself. In these cultures, if you propose with a very big engagement ring, your partner might not be comfortable with it (including wearing it) and might even question why you wasted so much money on it. In fact, I know people who never even had an engagement ring.

- **Preparing for marriage (Engaged):** As mentioned earlier, contrary to the Hugging Style, in the Kissing Style, people often embrace the process. Even though milestones (e.g., the proposal) are important, they don't put as much emphasis on them as they do in Hugging Style cultures.
  In the Kissing Style, it is not rare for couples to be in a relationship for ten years and never get married or be engaged for several years without a wedding in sight. However, the latter is a lot less common.

## When do they become official?

This is where it starts getting complicated because, contrary to the Hugging Style, where everything is so clearly structured (and talked about), in the Kissing Style, certain stages are assumed or do not have clear milestones. Namely:

- Exclusivity **1-1**

- Becoming official

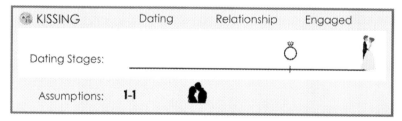

Becoming official in the Kissing Style

- **Exclusivity:** The Kissing Style can feel very easy-going due to the *assumed* exclusivity **1-1** from the start and the transition from the dating phase into the relationship (without a talk). One might feel they are already in a relationship while their "partner" is still deciding. As you are exclusive from the start, you can take your time until you feel ready.

- **Being official:** In the Kissing Style, becoming official 🏠
  happens at a different stage from becoming exclusive **1-1**.
  This is because, for them, exclusivity is the start. Therefore,
  as they haven't *yet* dated at the point when they become
  exclusive, they need some time to figure out their feelings
  and whether they are ready to start a relationship. Basically,
  they need time to date. Therefore, becoming official usually
  happens a few weeks after being exclusive.

### USA vs. FRANCE

*The one big difference was here in America [Hugging Style]
it's a big deal to ask a girl to be your girlfriend. It might and
usually includes small gifts, but you still specifically ask,
"Will you be my girlfriend?" Well, that wasn't the case.
He [Kissing Style] asked at some point if we were exclusive, and
when I said yes, apparently, that meant we were a couple. :D
He used the word 'girlfriend' later to refer to me, and I was like
oh?? It worked out in the end, but for a while, I was really
confused by our status. We still laugh about it when I told him we
specifically ask in the US, so he jokingly asked me formally many
months later. (Shelby)*

We can also see this with Antonio (Kissing Style) and Olivia
(Hugging Style). Antonio explained, "I started calling her my
girlfriend about a week after we started seeing each other."

Antonio's statement also reveals another big difference: becoming
official in the Kissing Style happens very subtly. They often don't
talk about it. Instead, they give clues that they consider each other
their girlfriend or boyfriend (though everyone is different – some
people are not as good at reading hints and ask, just to be on the
safe side).

*How do they give clues if they don't talk about it?*

I asked several of my friends from Kissing Style cultures how they do it, and we all had a very similar approach. We would often introduce someone as our partner (without discussing it with them in advance). So, for example, if I'm meeting my friend Anita, I'd introduce my partner and say to Anita: "This is my boyfriend, Antonio." . . . and if Antonio is not used to this, he might have a heart attack, but I'm sure he will recover :D

A Russian girl I met during my travels gave me a similar example. She said if someone invited her to a garden party, she might ask her partner in private: "Can I tell them my boyfriend is joining me?"

These are direct ways of telling the other person you consider them your partner, and they are supposed to get the message.

*What should you do if they introduce you as their partner?*

Whether you are ready for it or not, don't discuss it with your date in front of the third person; just go with the flow. You can talk about it later in private.

If you are also more than ready to call them your partner, you can refer to them later, maybe during a conversation with another person, as "my girlfriend/my boyfriend" in front of them, and they will be happy you returned it. Or, on the way home, you can comment in private so they know you've acknowledged it. For example, "It was nice of you to call me your boyfriend/girlfriend. I can't wait to introduce you like that, too." So, there are many different ways to do it subtly, without needing to have the awkward "What are we?" conversation.

If you are not ready yet, that's OK too. We are not always ready at the same time. Then, just wait till the evening is over and, on the way home, say something like, "It was really nice of you to introduce me as your girlfriend. I do enjoy your company, but I need a bit more time [to figure out how I feel]. Hope that's OK."

They will usually understand and wait for you to come around whenever you are ready. Normally, you will continue seeing each other like nothing has happened, as you want to get to know the person better. Whatever your reaction is, do acknowledge it one way or another (or return it), preferably on the same day, so they know where they stand.

Don't forget; this generally happens a week or two after you are exclusive (have kissed or had some chemistry). Don't introduce someone as your girlfriend or boyfriend out of the blue when you haven't had any type of romantic relationship with them. Otherwise, you will likely scare them off. You need some chemistry first!

*When you do not introduce them as your partner*

If you are dating someone from the Kissing Style, but you are not introducing them as your partner when they are expecting it, that can backfire, too! Just like it happened to a couple in Japan:

### ITALY vs. JAPAN

*Interestingly, in Japan, there is a precise moment when you move from casually hanging out with someone to being their girlfriend. They have to ask you: "Will you be my girlfriend?" My current boyfriend and I were having an evening out, and he introduced me to someone as his friend. I was distraught. I cried for about 30 minutes. He said: 'Oh no, I need to ask you properly, and you haven't said yes yet,' but in my mind, we were already official. In Italy, we start being committed in a relationship a lot sooner. We are missing that step.*[lxxiii]

It's easy to misunderstand dating cultures if you are not used to them, especially the Kissing Style. If you are unfamiliar with the Kissing Style and dating someone who is accustomed to it, you are better off playing it safe. Wait for them to hint at it first or try a very subtle conversation about it – especially to avoid awkwardly introducing them as a friend (e.g., "Do you think I could call you my girlfriend/boyfriend now?").

Do not rely purely on chemistry, without any kind of physical intimacy. People in these cultures tend to flirt a lot, and you might misread it as "chemistry" when they are just being nice. Often, people from cultures who hide their feelings can't differentiate between the two! Just like how Michael explained it earlier:

### GERMANY

> *As a German man, I don't make a lot of moves. If you feel interested, tell me. I'm not into misinterpreting being nice with flirting.* (Michael)

## Who should do it first?

Unlike in the Hugging Style, where men usually have to initiate the exclusivity talk, there is no such rule in the Kissing Style. Women often initiate the hint (especially because, in these cultures, women have the power at the beginning of the relationship, so they might take the lead).

## How long do they wait to say, "I love you"?

A user called debacchatio on Reddit replied to the question: "Do Brazilians [Kissing Style] say 'I love you' sooner when dating than Americans?" by saying his Brazilian partner [Kissing Style] said "I love you" after just three weeks of dating. He was really taken aback by this at the time, but it was eight years ago, and they are now happily married.[lxxiv]

A show on France 2, the national TV channel in France, stated that 8% of French people [Kissing Style] would feel comfortable confessing their love on the first date! Furthermore, according to the channel, many French people feel ready to say 'I love you' within just two months of meeting someone.[lxxv] This is very similar to my culture in Hungary, where I estimate it to be between a few weeks to two months also.

However, if we compare Hugging Style (masculine) and Kissing Style (feminine) cultures side by side, the difference is even greater, because Kissing Style cultures don't date. For them, the dating and relationship phases merge.

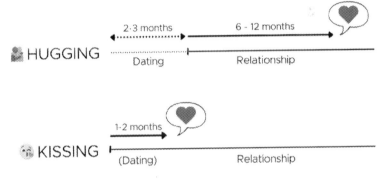

Therefore, while someone from a Kissing Style culture (who assumes exclusivity from the start) would be comfortable saying "I love you" within just two months of meeting their partner for the very first time, it could take someone from the Hugging Style as long as 8-15 months.

So why do people from Kissing Style cultures declare their love so early compared to the Hugging Style? This is partly because, in feminine cultures people usually feel emotions the most intensely in the early stages of dating. They never learned to hide (or control) their feelings. Therefore, they feel intense emotions at the start and then gradually calm down over time. Just like we saw it with their communication. But this is not the only reason.

As we know it, feminine cultures hate guessing games. However, contrary to the masculine Hugging Style, which has the exclusivity talk, in the Kissing Style, this step is missing. Hence, in the Kissing Style, until people confess their love to each other, there is no real confirmation of how serious they are. Expressing their love puts the other person at ease and eliminates the guessing game.

Therefore, if you are dating someone from a feminine culture, tell them when they are still questioning it in their head. Not when the answer feels obvious already. Saying it in the beginning when they need a little reassurance will make your relationship stronger.

You might think: if people in Kissing Style cultures say it so fast, they surely can't mean it. Some temperamental Latin American countries do have a reputation for that. However, even in Kissing Style cultures, not everyone is the same. Less temperamental feminine cultures like Hungary or France tend to show love through actions – for example, through chivalry, compliments, and romantic gestures instead of expressing it verbally. So, they are usually not throwing these words around.

Sylvia Sabes shares it in her article written for the BBC: "My French husband loves me." Sylvia knows it from her husband's actions. For example, he buys her flowers regularly, and he shows his love for her every day - even after a decade together. She then continues: "However, I can't remember the last time he said *'je t'aime'* (I love you)."[lxxvi]

Kissing Style cultures might say "I love you" comparably sooner to the Hugging Style, but the less temperamental ones will often go on for months or even years without saying it again. However, rest assured, it is totally normal, and it does not mean your partner does not love you anymore.

## Problems and Solutions

Now that we have some understanding of the Hugging and Kissing Styles, let's look at Olivia's and Antonio's problem.

The Hugging Style has three clearly defined phases: dating, relationship, and preparing for marriage (after the engagement). However, in the Kissing Style (to those who are not used to it), it can often feel like the dating phase is missing because they go exclusive from the start. So, when looking at the stages, it can feel like they only have two phases: the relationship phase and preparing for marriage. Even though the Kissing Style does have a dating phase, it starts after going exclusive, so their dating phase and relationship phase merge.

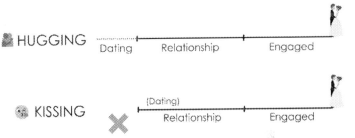

**Differences in dating stages of the Hugging vs. Kissing Styles**

This difference might seem tiny on paper, but it can cause all sorts of problems, to the point of putting someone off dating!

Just like in the case of Olivia and Antonio, Antonio was close to it.

**The Kissing Style** is common in Eastern European, Mediterranean, Latin American, and some African countries.

**Mindset:**

Society is slightly hierarchical, they show their feelings.

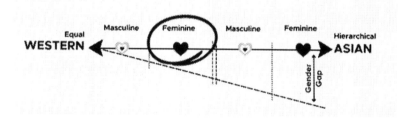

| Dating Stages: | Dating | Relationship | Engaged |
| --- | --- | --- | --- |

Dating Stages:

Assumptions:  1-1

# CHAPTER 11

# BOWING STYLE

## COUNTRIES WHERE IT IS COMMON

The Bowing Style is common in rather conservative countries, especially where Confucianism and Buddhism were historically the main religions, independent of how widely they are practiced today. These countries are mostly in East Asia.

**Countries with the Bowing Style**

## WHAT ARE THEIR MINDSETS & BELIEFS?

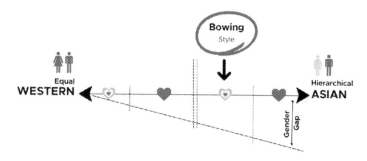

Before we look at their dating stages, let's review their mindset:

- **Men and women are not equal in society (hierarchical)**
    - They date with the aim to marry
    - Men pay on dates
    - They dress to impress – status is important
    - Introducing the parents usually means marriage
    - Getting their parents' approval is necessary

- **Society is success- and money-oriented; they hide their feelings**
    - Men have the power
    - They start with emotional intimacy
    - They don't play "hard to get" in a Western sense
    - Men impress their date with their achievements (job, money, education) and generosity, while women with their skills to be good mothers and housewives
    - They often date for two months
    - Communication: warms up slowly

##  WHAT ARE THEIR DATING STAGES?

Just like how Antonio was moving way too fast for Olivia, had Olivia dated someone with the Bowing Style, Olivia would have come across just as fast to them!

My Canadian friend Craig, who dated a Vietnamese girl, explained:

### CANADA vs. VIETNAM

> *In the beginning, everything went extremely slow compared to Canada. For the first two months, she [Vietnamese girl] would not even let me kiss her or hold her hand. Then, overnight, everything sped up. Suddenly she was introducing me to her family and all her friends and, three months into the relationship, started asking me about marriage. (Craig)*

Partially, this is because our fundamental definition of dating is different between Western and Asian dating cultures.

*Definition of "dating" in  Bowing Style countries*

In the Bowing Style, physical intimacy in premarital relationships is often frowned upon (though times are slowly changing). Therefore, the term "dating," which is of Western origin and assumed to imply certain expectations, including sexual interaction, often has a negative or even offensive connotation.

To reflect these cultural differences, we will call dating without any type of physical intimacy (including kissing and holding hands) 'courting.'

Let's look at the stages of Bowing style:

You will see that the Bowing Style is slightly similar to the Hugging Style in that it has a clear structure.

- **Courting/Dating** (phase)
- **Going public** 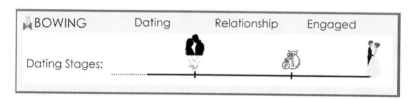 (milestone)
- **Relationship** (phase)
- **Engagement** (milestone)
- **Preparing for marriage/Engaged** (phase)

**Dating stages of the Bowing Style**

Let's look at them in detail:

- **Courting (Dating phase):** The dating phase (usually 1-2 months) is often fully focused on trying to find out whether the other person will be a suitable marriage partner. Usually, there is no touching or physical intimacy (not even kissing or holding hands).
  In many of these cultures, they often date in groups (purely due to being shy). If you are used to splitting the bill, get ready. . . here, men pay – even on group dates!

- **Going public ( ):** It is the moment you start holding hands (and often showing publicly that you are together). This can be shortly before or after you agree to become a couple. Usually, it is a good sign and often means the beginning of the relationship.

- **Relationship:** They assess whether they are a right fit for each other to get married, and when they feel ready, they introduce the family. Contrary to Western cultures, where meeting the parents normally does not mean anything, in the Bowing Style, it comes with a lot of pressure. It is one of the most fragile and vulnerable times because the couple needs the acceptance and approval of their family for their marriage.

  If their family disapproves, the couple usually have to break up, or occasionally, they run away and end their relationships with their families.

  Contrary to Western cultures, where the couple picks their own wedding day, in Asian cultures, usually the parents do. Therefore, if the parents agree for the couple to get married, the parents choose the engagement and the wedding day with the help of a fortune teller. (Most Asian cultures are very superstitious, therefore significant events have to be on a "lucky day.")

- **Engagement ( ):** Customarily, in Asian cultures, the daughter is the property of the father. Hence, she can't accept a proposal.

  Instead, in these cultures, the man goes to the girl's parents' house to ask for their approval for marriage and pays the bride price (or dowry in some cultures, depending on whether it is paid by the bride or the groom's family).

  The bride price or dowry is either money or gifts – often agreed upon by the families in advance. Once they hand over the bride price/dowry, the engagement is official.

  This tradition exists even in more developed Asian countries like China and South Korea.

**China** is one of the few countries where a compulsory bride price and voluntary dowry co-exist.

However, in recent years, partially due to China's one-child policy between 1979-2015 and its deep cultural preference for boys, bride prices - called cǎilǐ (彩礼) or pìnlǐ (聘礼), that the groom's family should offer to the bride's family, have skyrocketed. Back in 2013, the highest bride price paid included a house and approx. $15,000. The situation is the worst in rural areas, where in 2014, men had to save an average of 12 years of income to afford the bride price, but these figures even doubled in 2017. Now, many men in China cannot afford a bride.[lxxvii]

### The situation is similar in South Korea.

Han Gyoung Hae, a professor of family studies at Seoul National University, explains that "If, traditionally, the gifts were meant to tie families together, now they are meant to show off how rich you are."[lxxviii]

Some couples even break up before they tie the knot, if the bridegroom's family is not happy with the dowry.

The situation got so bad that the Korean government even started to pay a subsidy to Korean men marrying foreign brides to save its shrinking population. "Foreign brides are often 'bought' from developing Asian countries such as Vietnam, Cambodia, and the Philippines," explains Mustika Hapsoro in his article written for Vice's website.[lxxix]

- **Preparing for marriage/Engaged:** In traditional families, the preparation can be several months prior to the wedding. However, nowadays, it is usually just 1-2 weeks. The engagement and the wedding are often held on the same day (for convenience).

## *When Do They Become Official?*

Even though referring to each other as girlfriend/boyfriend is a clear step in the process, it comes with underlying assumptions.

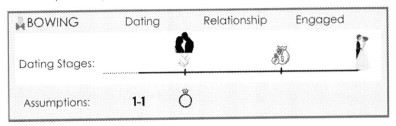

- **Exclusivity:** They typically date non-exclusively initially, then either gradually assume or talk about dating exclusively **1-1**.

  (In Vietnam, exclusivity is usually assumed, while in Korea and Japan, they often talk about it.)

- **Preparing for marriage (Assumption):** Once the couple goes public and starts the relationship, they naturally assume they will get married – unless something goes wrong. In these cultures, dating for "fun" is considered a waste of time; they date to marry. Hence, going public is not only about becoming official but also the equivalent of the proposal in Western countries – even though it is only assumed! There is no engagement ring. This is why there is often a lot of pressure in the Bowing Style when it comes to dating someone.

  Contrary to Western cultures, where the couple doesn't know whether they will get married until the proposal, in Asian cultures, they naturally assume it from the start. Traditionally, in these cultures, there is no proposal – at least not in a Western sense. If they do have one with an engagement ring, it is only symbolic (taken from Western cultures), but not a "YES or NO" deciding event.

*How long do they wait to say, "I love you"?*

Dating in Asia can be very confusing to Westerners because even if the Asian person is interested, they often won't kiss or hold someone's hand. This is because, in Asian cultures, a love confession comes before anything else.

In Japan, for example, it is called the act of kokuhaku – confessing your love and asking someone to go out with you.
A typical kokuhaku may sound like:

> "I love you. Can we start seeing each other?"[lxxx]

When a foreign person asks about the chance of going out on another date and a Japanese person replies, "Of course, what is it?" they may be expecting your kokuhaku – explains Mami Suzuki from Japan in her blog post. "The love confession is like a switch. Once the switch is flipped, they can get into relationship mode." Therefore, generally, they won't behave like a girlfriend or boyfriend until they are formally dating.[lxxxi]

You might go on a few dates, but you are not officially in a relationship until the confession happens. Confession is an important step in Asian cultures because they believe "You should be committed if you want to be with someone." They date to marry. Hence, confessing your love is a crucial step for a romantic relationship to begin in many Asian cultures.

An article about dating in Taiwan explains that before the confession occurs, the connection is purely one of being friends or liking each other. Yet, suddenly, when the love confession happens, that means there is a commitment to date with the intention of getting married.[lxxxii]

An article in The Korea Herald explains that in South Korea: "Only when one party makes the confession, the so-called 'some' stage [dating stage] ends and the two become a couple."[lxxxiii]

Duc Nguyen confirms it is the same in Vietnam: "When you think you're ready for a committed relationship, confess your love to her." He explains you can only take things further physically if you're in a committed relationship with your partner.[lxxxiv]

In most Asian cultures, dating for fun (without the intention of getting married in the near future) is viewed as a waste of time. Hence, some adults in Japan even choose to confess in the following way:

"I would like to have a relationship with you with the objective of an eventual marriage."[lxxxv]

Mami Suzuki explains that in Japan, the thought of starting a relationship can be so overwhelming that people might even 'confess their love' before the first date.[lxxxvi]

However, Japan is not the only place! Lauren from the UK ghosted a Taiwanese man called Mike due to this cultural difference. After just two weeks of talking online, Mike confessed his love to Lauren and asked her to be his girlfriend. Lauren felt insulted:

"I just don't understand. Before that text, everything was going so well. I could see myself dating Mike in a week if he had asked me out. But then he rushed it like this, making me feel pressured, let alone it was cringy and creepy."[lxxxvii]

Even though confessing in Asia is a significant milestone that marks the beginning of the relationship, the term "I love you" doesn't have the same meaning as it does in the West. A Reddit user called Interesting_Carrot26 explained that: "'I love you' doesn't really have a significant meaning in Korea. Same significance as saying, 'I miss you'."[lxxxviii]

Therefore, keep these cultural differences in mind when sharing your feelings with your partner or if hearing their love confession just doesn't feel right.

**The Bowing Style** is common in East Asian countries.

**Mindset:**

Society is hierarchical, they hide their feelings.

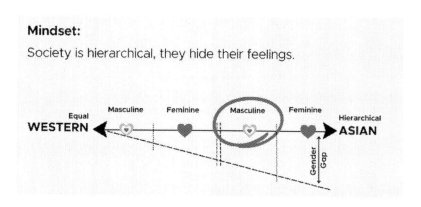

**Dating Stages:**

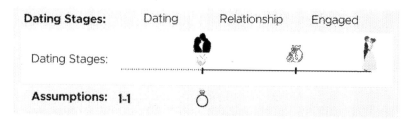

# CHAPTER 12

# ○ TRADITIONAL STYLE

## COUNTRIES WHERE IT IS COMMON

Traditional Style dating culture is especially common where Islam and Hinduism were historically the main religions, independent of how widely they are practiced today. Furthermore, it is also practiced within some conservative religious groups, e.g., among Hasidic Jews – a subgroup of Judaism.

It can be found in South Asian countries, on the Arabian Peninsula, and the African continent, plus among many immigrant families in the West.

**Countries with the Traditional Style**

## ⬭ WHAT ARE THEIR MINDSETS & BELIEFS?

Let's review their mindset:

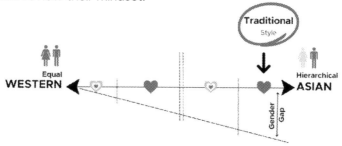

- **Men and women are not equal in society (very hierarchical)**
    - They have arranged marriages: a marriage partner is often selected and introduced by the parents.
    - Marriage is a means of achieving financial stability.
    - Virginity is usually a prerequisite for marriage.

- **Society is people-oriented; they show their feelings**
    - Men have the power.
    - Usually, love—if they are lucky—develops after marriage.
    - Sexual intimacy outside of wedlock is not only frowned upon, but especially in Islamic countries, it is a criminal offence and often punished with a prison sentence of several years or even death penalty.

Please note, in Islamic countries, Do not flirt with, hit on, touch, hug, or talk privately to women. IT COULD ENDANGER THEIR SAFETY![lxxxix]

# ⌀ WHAT ARE THEIR DATING STAGES?

People with the Traditional Style typically marry within their community. Even though you are less likely to end up in an intercultural relationship with them, as the world becomes more global and many people from Traditional style cultures study in Western countries, we will cover it just in case you need it.

Although Islam and Hinduism have opposing beliefs, they have a similar approach to relationships. However, due to their opposite religions, they don't intermarry or eat together – even though in Islam, Muslim men are allowed to marry "the people of the holy books", which includes Christians and Jews. Marrying Hindus is prohibited by the religion.

A Muslim* man who married a Hindu woman in India is one of the few exceptions. He shared his story:

### MUSLIM – HINDU MARRIAGE

*I'm happily married to a woman I love, and we have a wonderful daughter. Was it hard to go against the parents' will? Well, I did. She did. It's not common here in India; you really need to have the guts to do so. My family was not happy, but we didn't lose connection. My wife's family disowned her, and they hadn't seen each other for a very long time. It took several years until they met us again just in order to see their granddaughter and my relatives.* (Shaan)

*Islam is the religion, and people who follow Islam are called Muslims.

Traditional Style countries (both Hindu and Muslim) usually have arranged marriages. The general purpose of arranged and sometimes even forced marriages "is for families to be selective about who their children marry as a way to control familial relations and extensions", explains an article on New Idea's website.[xc]

In some cases, they are also viewed as a symbolic gesture to strengthen mergers and partnerships in the realms of business and politics or to gain wealth, status, or reputation. Occasionally, they are even agreed upon while the bride and groom are still infants.

Traditional Style is the only dating style out of the four where the relationship phase is missing. Mohsina explains:

### LOVE IN ISLAM

*Islam doesn't prohibit something natural. Love or romance is allowed between spouses after marriage. But it is not allowed among non-married men and women as it would encourage fornication and adultery, which is a big sin in Islam.*[xci]

Therefore, in Muslim countries, it is illegal for men and women to live together, share a hotel room, or even for an unmarried woman to be pregnant out of wedlock. The consequences can include jail, deportation, or physical punishment.

Even if you don't travel to a Muslim country but are dating someone from one of these countries, it is important to be aware of this!

ABC News shared the story of Jared Al-Jasser Morrison, whose American mother dated a Saudi man who was studying in the US.[xcii] They met at university in the 70s. However, when Jared's mother became pregnant, his father returned to Saudi Arabia, where one's reputation and family honor are more important than anything else. Brietta Hague, from ABC News, explains that "Jared's father would have been ostracized by his family and society had he married a foreigner and non-Muslim."

When I reached out to Jared, he was extremely kind to share his story and give some advice. He highlighted that there are religious values, and cultural values, but on top of it all, family/tribal pressure is often even more significant.

He explained that "They [Saudi Arabian men] behave very differently in the US than when they go back home. They change. So go and see. Make sure you meet the family!" If they don't introduce you, they are not serious about you.

Jared also shared an interesting insight: "In Saudi Arabia [and in most Muslim countries], men and women don't mix. They have separate living quarters in the house, and even schools are separate. They can't go on dates like people do in Western countries."

Consequently, due to the culture and social pressure, Jared grew up without a father, and he is not alone. Saudi men abroad continue to father and abandon children, sometimes despite promising the woman marriage and a life together.

ABC News explained that Saudi Arabia's strict Sharia law makes it impossible for students to marry foreign women. They need the Government's permission, and only men over 30 can apply.

However, it's important to separate Islam from the culture. Islam doesn't prohibit marrying foreigners, as long as they are people of the holy book (Christians or Jews), but Saudi Arabia's culture does.

Many women and their children are now trying to find their fathers with the help of a blog called 'Saudi Children Left Behind'.

Of course, there are many Muslim men who would never abandon their children, and men abandon children in Western countries, too. However, when it comes to Muslim countries, it is important to be aware that it can happen due to the culture and Islam's view on fornication, which is that it is a huge sin.

Through a Western cultural lens, we might only judge the men, but via the lens of Islam, women are just as guilty and share the sin with the runaway fathers of having an unmarried relationship.

Let's look at the stages of the Traditional Style:

- **Engagement** 💰 (milestone)
- **Preparing for marriage/Engaged** (phase)

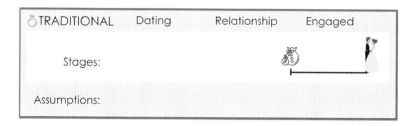

Dating stages of the Traditional Style

Let's look at them in detail:

- **Engagement** (💰):

  **In Hindu marriage:** The tradition of a dowry is still alive, even though according to modern laws, it is illegal in some countries (e.g., India). However, parents may still propose dowry for their daughter, but now they call it "a gift."

  **In Islamic marriage:** Milson Legal Solicitors explain that a 'mahr' is a gift that the bride receives from the groom. It can be something non-material, such as teaching her to read the Qur'an. It has no specified value. However, it is the bride's right to receive something and it is essential to form a marriage contract. Otherwise, the marriage is not valid.[xciii]

Some people confuse mahr with a bride price and a dowry, but there is a big difference between them! In his article on Questions on Islam, Mehmet Paksu explains the differrence[xciv]:

**Mahr** is a present given directly from the groom to the bride upon marriage.

**A bride price** is the amount of money that the bride's father wants for himself as the price for his daughter.

**A dowry** is the money that the father of the girl pays to the bridegroom (and his family) for marrying his daughter.

Mr. Paksu explains that "Money demanded from the would-be groom [the bride price] turns marriage into a matter of financial bargaining" – just like the dowry.

- **Preparing for Marriage**:

**In Islam:** "The people to be married can see each other only when people go and ask the girl's parents for her hand in marriage",[xcv] says Mr. Paksu. Otherwise, the couple cannot see or talk to each other unless they make a marriage contract. Even if they are engaged, it is only appropriate for the couple to meet and talk if a "mahram" is present. A mahram is a person's sibling, parent, grandparent, uncle/aunt, or nephew/niece. Therefore, if there is any kind of courting, it is usually done in groups, so the two people are not left alone together.

Mostafa Hassan, a Muslim man, explained that the engagement phase is actually the time when the couple can get to know each other, but only through talking."[xcvi]

**In urban areas of India (Hindu),** according to India Today, "future spouses are often expected to go out on dates and develop a romantic relationship in the period between their engagement and their wedding."[xcvii] In more conservative rural areas, a limited amount of interaction, or even romantic courtship, between the man and woman follows. "Dating may not be socially permissible; nonetheless, the couple may talk over the phone"[xcviii] Indian Anthropological Association shares it in their Journal, the Indian Anthropologist.

Please note that arranged and forced marriages are NOT the same!

- **Arranged marriages:** Usually, the parents or grandparents select the bride or groom, often with the help of a marriage broker (matchmaker). The potential partners are then introduced to each other. In arranged marriages, the parties have some level of choice in whom they choose to marry.

- **Forced marriages:** On the other hand, a forced marriage is imposed on the couple, entirely against their wishes. They don't have the option to decline it and often barely meet their partner prior to the wedding day – if at all. They might meet each other once, for 30 minutes or even less.

  The practices of dowry and bride price contribute to forced marriages – which are often the result of[xcix]:

  - **Bride kidnapping** – where the woman is kidnapped and often raped by the groom-to-be, so the man can negotiate the bride price as she is not a virgin. In most circumstances, the future bride then has no choice but to accept, or there will be so much shame on her family as she is 'impure.'
  - **Unplanned pregnancy**
  - **Settling the debts** of the girl's parents.

- o **Dispute resolution** – where the conflict is 'resolved' by one of the families giving a female to the other.

Dowry is considered to be one of the main reasons for violence against women in India. In some cases, dowry is used as a threat to be able to demand more property from the bride's family, which is called dowry harassment. Often, the bride's family has no other option to protect their daughter but to give more dowry.[c] Hence why a dowry is illegal in India.

Finally, in Islam, they also have so-called "temporary marriages" - a practice that few in the West know about. Even though it is so unique, I am going to explain it because this is a way someone from another culture could have a relationship with and marry someone with the Traditional Style.

- **Temporary marriages**: Nikah mut'ah (or "pleasure marriage") is an ancient Islamic practice when a man marries a woman for a specific length of time—it can be as short as a few hours or last several months or years—and expires at the end of the marriage contract. The contract states the time frame of the marriage and the mahr that the man has to pay to the woman, and it can also include stipulations (e.g., no physical intimacy).
  There are opposing views on temporary marriage among Muslims; Shia Muslims practice it, while Sunni Muslims consider it haram – forbidden.

In a 30-minute BBC documentary called "Married for a Minute,"[ci] Islamic scholars say temporary marriage is on the rise among Shia students, especially on university campuses in England and Wales.

In Islam, dating and "romantic, intimate relationships are prohibited before marriage."[cii]

Sara, a 30-year-old Shia Muslim of Pakistani heritage living in the UK, explained it in her interview with the BBC. Temporary marriage allowed her and her husband to meet without breaking the rules of Sharia, the Islamic law. They both wanted to date and to get to know each other before getting married, which would have been impossible otherwise.

On the other hand, Khola Hassan, a Sunni Muslim, explained that temporary marriage is prohibited because it is equal to prostitution. "There is a time limit on the marriage, and the mahr given as a gift is the equivalent as a payment to a prostitute."

There are greatly opposing views on temporary marriages, and it is often considered a taboo and haram (forbidden). However, it is important to be aware of it. Jared's mum had to raise him alone after his father disappeared back to Saudi Arabia without marrying her. However, you could end up in the same situation if you unknowingly enter into a temporary marriage. According to Arab News, many women "do not know that their marriages would end within a few days and that they would have to bear children of people who would abandon them."[ciii] These women often can't even get spouse visas to enter the husband's country because temporary marriages are not registered. Therefore, if someone asks you for a temporary marriage, educating yourself on the differences is important, particularly in areas such as your rights to children (which in a mut'ah marriage are the rights of the father).

Even though temporary marriages in many Muslim countries are illegal, you might still come across them in Shia Muslim countries like Iran and among Shia Muslims living in the West.

## Generational Clashes

Before the spread of Western influence in Asia and the Middle East, arranged marriages were the norm. Even though this still remains true in many cultures, in some others—like Pakistan and Turkey, and among immigrant families in the West—younger generations are now starting to find their own partners. However, older generations still often reject the idea of "dating" because, due to its Western origin, it is associated with premarital sex. Therefore, many young Muslims now refer to it as *halal dating*.

In his article published on NPR's news website, Neha Rashid explains that "Halal refers to something permissible within Islam. Some couples argue that by adding the permissibility factor, they are removing the idea that anything *haram*, or prohibited, such as premarital sex, is happening in the relationship." To avoid misunderstandings, people in Muslim communities often prefer to avoid the word dating altogether and refer to it as: "talking" or "getting to know each other."[civ]

Therefore, what is borrowed from the Western term "dating" is that people now choose their own partner while still keeping their cultural and religious values – usually including not engaging in physical intimacy until marriage.

**The Traditional Style** is common in South Asian countries on the Arabian Peninsula, and the African continent.

**Mindset:**

Society is very hierarchical, they show their feelings.

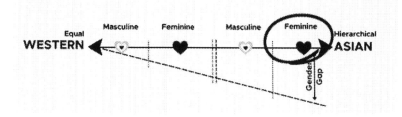

**Dating Stages:**     Dating     Relationship     Engaged

Dating Stages:

**Assumptions:**    NO ASSUMPTIONS

COMPREHENSIV
OVERVIEW

Understanding individual dating styles –
how people from different cultures think and
behave – was our foundation. However, to
help you easily navigate them, in the following
chapters we will focus on comparing them.

# CHAPTER 13

# COMPARISON OF DATING STAGES

Now that we have covered all the dating styles, let's circle back to their mindsets for a moment, where we discussed how Western cultures date to find love while Asian cultures date to marry.

When people from Western cultures start dating people from the Asian Bowing Style, both parties often believe they are in a different stage of the relationship once they are exclusive.

People used to the Hugging or Kissing Style believe they are in the *relationship phase* (figuring out whether the person is right for them to marry). However, the person used to the Bowing Style believes they will get married, unless something goes wrong. Hence, in a Western sense, the Bowing Style assumes they are "engaged."

Even though the Bowing Style has clearly defined stages, for those who are used to one of the other dating styles, especially the Hugging Style, it can give the feeling of being extremely slow in the beginning. Then suddenly, everything speeds up, and it becomes one of the fastest of the four.

If we look at its dating stages, it's easy to understand why. What is known as the relationship phase in Western cultures is merged with being engaged in the Bowing Style. They have the courting phase, and then, once the couple becomes official (which is referring to each other as girlfriend/boyfriend and the assumed proposal combined), they start assessing whether they should get married. So, the moment they begin the relationship, in a Western sense, it is more like jumping ahead to the proposal. Their relationship phase feels as if it is part of being engaged.

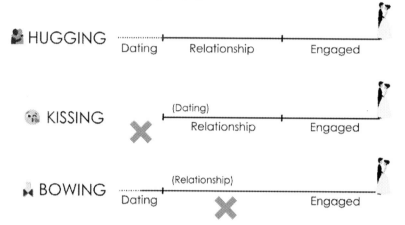

**Differences in dating stages of the Hugging, Kissing, and Bowing Styles**
**(Traditional Style is not included, as they do not date)**

This is why, in many countries with the Bowing Style, people have far fewer dating partners than those in Western cultures. In fact, they often marry their first girlfriend or boyfriend, especially if they live in the countryside, which is usually more traditional than dating in cities.

## How long is the dating phase?

We can see an interesting pattern if we compare cultures' dating stages based on whether they hide or show their feelings. Cultures that hide their feelings (the masculine Hugging and Bowing Styles) date for around two months before starting a relationship. They take time to figure out how they feel about each other and whether they want to be in a relationship with the person. On the contrary, cultures that are in touch with their feelings and show it (the feminine Kissing Style), fast-track to the relationship by skipping the dating phase.

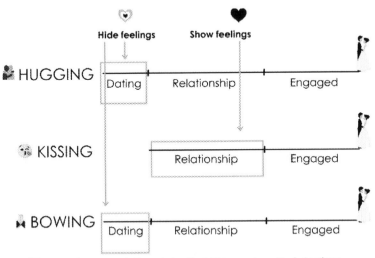

**Difference between dating styles that hide or show their feelings**

## USA

> *The question of when to have the exclusivity talk can be a stressful thing in the American dating scene. It can be awkward if you bring it up before the other person is ready, but you also don't want to invest too much of your time in someone who isn't going to commit.* (Peter)

## FRANCE vs. SWEDEN

> I find it fascinating how in France, you naturally become a couple after about three dates. In Sweden, it usually takes much longer and a lot more dates before you decide you're in a relationship. (Sofi)

## ITALY

> *Exclusivity is the norm; the concept itself doesn't really exist because it's a given. If you ask a person out multiple times, that person automatically thinks he/she has all the cards to officially be your partner.* (Enrico)

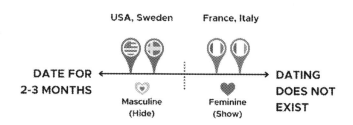

**Differences in length of dating phase**

In masculine cultures, where people hide their feelings, they often take a long time to recognize how they feel about each other and reveal it to start a relationship. They often date for two months or even longer – because they need time to figure out their feelings.

A survey of 1000 adults carried out by global market research firm Ipsos, revealed that "39% of the participants thought three months was a good time frame before becoming exclusive."[cv]

As it often works out to be approximately 10 dates (1 date/week), it is often called the 10-date rule.

On the contrary, in feminine cultures, where people naturally show (and know) how they feel, they often fast-track to the relationship – and it feels as if they skipped dating altogether.

# CHAPTER 14

# CROSSOVER BETWEEN DATING STYLES

We are familiar with transitions between cultures and their mindsets, but now let's look at how it affects dating styles, as there is a similar pattern:

**Liberal** ⟵————————⟶ **Conservative**

| 🧍 Hugging | 😗 Kissing | 🙇 Bowing | 💍 Traditional |
|---|---|---|---|
| • Physical intimacy is the start | • Emotional intimacy is the start | | • Virginity is a pre-requisitite |
| • Emotional intimacy comes later | • Physical intimacy comes later | | |
| • Dates before exclusivity | • Dates after exclusivity | • Dates before exclusivity (courting) | |
| • Dates to find love | • Dates to find love | • Dates to marry | • Marriage is the start |
| • Often date more people before marriage | • Often date more people before marriage | • Often marry their first partner | • Marry their first partner |
| • Plans for children later (2 yrs+ into the relationship) | • Plans for children later (2 yrs+ into the relationship) | • Plans for children as early as (3-6 month+ into the relationship) | • Wants children very early (3 months into the relationship) |

**Characteristics of Dating Styles**

Even though there are these four distinctively different dating styles with contrasting characteristics, we can often find "mixtures" of them.

A person with a bit more conservative Hugging Style may show some characteristics of the Kissing Style.

For example, in Sweden, even though they are used to the Hugging Style, where they date slowly until they become more and more comfortable with the other person, dating often turns into a relationship without a talk – which is typical of the less structured Kissing Style.

### SWEDEN

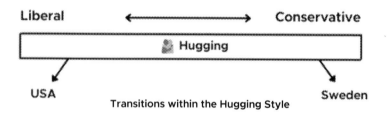

*The concept of dating doesn't exist in Sweden.*
*"We don't really do formal dating in Nordic countries."*[cvi]
*"Swedes are very informal that way; we simply hang out, and if we like each other, things sort of develop organically."*[cvii]

Liberal ⟷ Conservative

Hugging

USA                                        Sweden

**Transitions within the Hugging Style**

Someone with a more conservative Kissing Style might kiss and hold hands in public but wait for more physical intimacy until marriage. Or they might start planning for children and marriage very fast, 3-4 months into the relationship. This is considered way too fast in many Kissing Style cultures, but rather normal in many Bowing Style cultures.

Liberal  ⟷  Conservative

| Kissing |
|---|

France        Eastern European        Sub-Saharan
              countries               African countries

**Transitions within the Kissing Style**

France is one of the most liberal Kissing style cultures, whereas many African countries are on the more conservative side of the spectrum. African countries focus on marriage and having children a lot sooner - which is seen in the West as a more conservative practice.

Furthermore, contrary to most Kissing Style cultures where men and women inherit equally, in many Kissing Style African cultures (e.g., Kenya), only men inherit. This makes their society very similar to the Bowing Style, where the man's family is expected to pay a bride price, which is not a tradition in typical Kissing Style cultures.

On the other hand, nowadays, in some liberal Bowing Style cultures like Japan, only very traditional, often rural, families still practice the tradition of "Yuinou kin" (engagement money). However, the concept is very different from the bride price because "it is given by the groom-to-be's family to the bride-to-be family for her to get ready with the furniture to leave home."[cviii]

Even though the tradition of a bride price is gradually disappearing, they still date to marry, and men still need to ask the girl's parents for their approval. In his article posted on Tofugu's website, Nathan says, "You don't absolutely have to, but many Japanese fathers would be insulted if you didn't."[cix]

In Kenya, where men often spend exorbitant amounts on a bride price, an article on Nairobi News promotes marrying Japanese women in their article titled, *Can't afford bride price? Japan is the place to be.*

They explain: "Apparently, all it requires for a man to secure a lifetime partner is to convince the lady in question that he, indeed, is madly in love with her."[cx]

Furthermore, someone with a more liberal Bowing Style might have more relationships and even physical intimacy before marriage or going public. However, they are still likely to focus on marriage and family very quickly (a few months) after starting a relationship.

This transition is also present in Traditional Style. Hindus, especially those living in big cities, are on the more liberal end of the spectrum, while Muslim cultures are on the more conservative side.

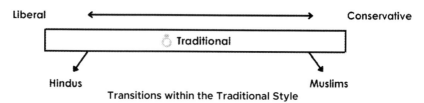

Transitions within the Traditional Style

## INDIA

> *Most marriages in India are arranged. But I know many metropolitan Indians who are in the cities like Pune, Mumbai, Delhi, etc., who date and have 'love marriages.' Or they date for a while and then end up having an arranged marriage anyway. They meet on apps like Tinder, Hinge, Bumble, etc., or meet at work, or through friends, or at cafes/bars. This is the minority of people, though, as the majority of the population is very traditional still.*
>
> (Joan - dated an Indian man)

Those who *date* in Traditional Style cultures date like the Bowing Style, but as Joan explained, they might still have an arranged marriage at the end, which is typical of the Traditional Style.

## HIJAB IN ISLAM

*In Islam, wearing a hijab [head scarf] is compulsory so that Muslim women can be distinguished and taken care of by Muslim men like their own sisters and daughters, and so their beauty and body are not objectified by other men.* (Nazia)

In most countries, Muslim women have a choice whether to cover up or not. Some wear it out of respect for their religion, some for their culture while others wear it as a fashion item. Don't automatically assume they are religious or label them as conservative or oppressed. However, in a few Traditional style countries, women (whether locals or foreigners - regardless of their religion) don't have the choice. In these countries (e.g., Iran – where a hijab is mandatory, or Afghanistan, where the Burka is), women's attire often reflects the country's conservative values:

Liberal ←——————————————→ Conservative

Hijab    Chador    Niqab    Burka

Sometimes, you can see this crossover even within one country. For example, the USA has a region called "The Bible Belt," where people tend to be more conservative in their values. Contrary to most parts of the US, where people usually split the bill, in the Bible Belt, men often pay.

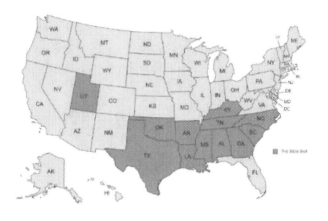

**The "Bible Belt" in the USA**[cxi]

Extreme shifts among dating styles are less likely.

Someone with a more conservative Hugging Style might show characteristics of the Kissing Style but is unlikely to show elements of the very conservative Bowing Style (like marrying their first partner and trying for children within months).

Additionally, there are generational differences within each of these dating styles. While many aspects of the dating style remain the same, *younger generations tend to be more liberal.* Even though they usually keep the same dating style, they shift within it from the conservative to the more liberal end.

We are all different, but once you are familiar with the four dating styles, slight differences between them become easy to navigate.

# CHAPTER 15

# CONFUSIONS & MISUNDERSTANDINGS

## DATING

*Are you official?*

People who are used to the Hugging Style often ask, "Are you official?" but for those who are used to the Kissing Style, this can be confusing if they are in the dating phase. Why?

In the Hugging Style, "Are you official?" means:

"Are you exclusive **1-1** and referring to each other as your girlfriend or boyfriend?" Therefore, are you in a relationship? (See arrow #1)

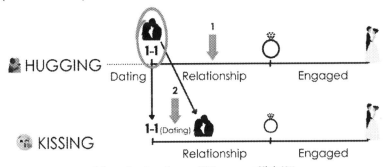

**Misunderstandings of "Are you official?"**

However, in the Kissing Style, if the person is in the dating phase, they will be between the two. They will be exclusive already **1-1**, but they won't yet be ready to call their partner their boyfriend or girlfriend ♟(See arrow #2). This is because they are in the dating phase and not in the relationship phase.

The relationship starts after you refer to each other as your girlfriend or boyfriend ♟, not before.

Therefore, if a person in the Hugging Style asks, "Are you official?" often, the person in the Kissing Style will still say "yes": they are official as they are exclusive (arrow pointing to the exclusivity talk **1-1**).

However, according to the Hugging Style, that would not count as "official," as the person is not calling their partner their girlfriend or boyfriend. That happens after the dating phase (arrow pointing to ♟). Therefore, as they are in the dating phase, they are still deciding whether they want to be official.

So, if you are used to the Hugging Style and looking to date someone from the Kissing Style, try to ask the question differently, or you might think they are in a relationship when they are not quite yet.

Instead of asking, "Are you official?" ask, "Are they your boyfriend or girlfriend?" The answers might be very different!

## *"Are You Exclusive?" or "Dating Exclusively"?*

Once I was already aware of cultural differences in dating, I tried to explain my Kissing Style dating culture to some American friends (Hugging Style); however, we got stuck at the dating phase.

I explained: "In the US, people date multiple people, but in my culture, we date exclusively."

One of my American friends replied: "I usually date exclusively too."

I knew we were talking about different things, but I was struggling to explain it.

### What was I getting wrong?

"Dating Exclusively" or "Being Exclusive" is not the same thing.

"Dating Exclusively" refers to the *dating phase*.

Meanwhile, "Being Exclusive" means you had "the talk," *the milestone* **1-1** (or assumed it), and you are now in an exclusive relationship.

### In the Hugging Style (e.g., USA):

"Dating exclusively" is a personal choice/preference (See arrow #1). At this stage, the person has not talked about "being exclusive" with his/her partner yet.

"Being exclusive" **1-1** happens at a later stage.

HUGGING — Dating — Relationship — Engaged

## On the contrary, in the Kissing Style:

"Being exclusive" **1-1** is assumed from the start without a talk. Therefore, "dating exclusively" (arrow #2) is not a choice. It is given.

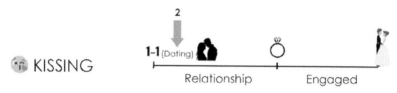

For people who are used to the Kissing Style, as they date *after* being exclusive **1-1**, "dating exclusively" usually means the same thing as "being exclusive." They can't differentiate between the two.

### *"Homewrecker" or Serious?*

A few years ago, when I asked one of my friends from New Zealand: "How long are you supposed to chase a girl (if at all) after she says she has a boyfriend," the answer I got was:

> *What . . .??? How long am I going to chase a girl who told me that she's got a boyfriend??? Hmmmmm... NOT AT ALL!!! Why the hell should anyone chase someone who's not single?!*
> (Blake)

In his Hugging Style dating culture, when someone goes exclusive, they start the relationship. There is a clear cut between the dating phase and the relationship phase. If someone is chasing once the person is in a relationship, they might be accused of being a "homewrecker," breaking up the relationship. Of course, we are all different, but in the Hugging Style, as soon as someone is exclusive with somebody else, in most cases, they stop chasing.

On the other hand, in the Kissing and Bowing Style, if you stop chasing the person once they are exclusive with someone else, it means you are not serious about them.

In the Kissing Style, as we looked at it earlier, being exclusive doesn't mean you are referring to each other as boyfriend and girlfriend. That usually happens a few weeks later. In those few weeks, there is a fairly high chance you will "break up." In these cultures, knowing what you want and going for it (especially in relationships) is considered very attractive. Therefore, men often chase women for 1-3 months even after she has started seeing someone. It means they are serious about her. If she happens to become single and the man was her "Plan B" in the queue, she might give him a chance. However, if he disappeared, she would think he was not serious. He gave up at the first hurdle and was not willing to work for what he wanted.

Similarly, in the Bowing Style, men often chase for 1-2 years to prove that they are serious. In the Bowing Style, they date to marry, and they usually get married within 1-2 years. So, men chase during that period.

Therefore, if you are used to the Hugging Style and want to date someone who is used to the Kissing or Bowing Style, keep this in mind. If you don't chase them to prove you are serious, they will likely never date you - even if they become single in the future.

*Are you back in the game?*

Those who are used to the Hugging Style occasionally ask, "Are you back in the game?" They are referring to the dating phase when you are dating others, but you are not official with anyone (See arrow #1).

However, for those who are used to the Kissing Style, this question can be very confusing. Let's look at why.

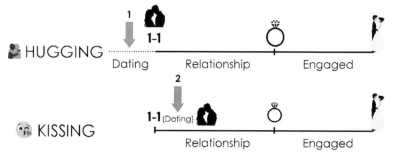

Misunderstandings of "Are you back in the game?"

In the Kissing Style, as they are exclusive **1-1** from the start, they can't really call it "back in the game," as it would suggest they are seeing multiple people while they are exclusive, which is considered cheating (See arrow #2).

Therefore, in the Kissing Style, they are not "back in the game." The closest to it would be when they are single, prior to going exclusive **1-1** with someone. However, it is not the same. During that time, they couldn't be any more single.

In the Kissing Style, being single or dating someone exclusively can often change in an afternoon. There is no time for "in the game" between.

This can also be a misunderstanding between the Bowing Style and Kissing Style (as in the Bowing Style, the dating phase is also prior to exclusivity, just like it is in the Hugging Style).

## CHEATING

Cheating is a serious issue on its own, let alone when it is purely based on misunderstandings! You might be wondering, "How can cheating be purely due to misunderstandings?"

In the Hugging Style, as you are not exclusive with anyone in the dating phase, seeing multiple people doesn't count as cheating.

In contrast, in the Kissing Style, as they assume exclusivity from the start (without even talking about it), if you date multiple people, it counts as cheating. You might think that problems that arise from cultural differences can be remedied by discussing them later. However, these beliefs are so deeply rooted that what's done usually can't be undone. So don't take them lightly.

Unfortunately, I had my own personal experience with this. Let me explain so you don't have to learn it at your own cost. It happened once I was already aware of this cultural difference, but it still didn't play out well.

Before we look at the issue in detail, let me clarify: this section is not to blame anyone. It's purely to help you understand the cultural differences in play and what you should look out for if you end up in a similar situation.

This is what happened: I met an American guy, and I explained to him that in my dating culture, we go exclusive from the start; therefore, it is not OK with me to date multiple people. He told me this is how it is in the US, even if he doesn't like it.

So, what happened? I assumed that because he stated he didn't like it and we talked about it, he would not do it – date multiple people. However, he did, which felt like I was stabbed in the back.

In my eyes, he lied because he still did it (even though he "didn't like it") and cheated because we agreed(?).

Apparently, we did not agree.

In the Hugging Style, communication has to be very clear. They say what they mean, and mean what they say – exactly as we can see in the dating stages of the Hugging Style. Very clear and structured. (I felt I did my part just by explaining our cultural differences to him and assumed that the discussion meant we were exclusive.)

In my Kissing Style dating culture (and across my culture in general), we often read between the lines. We don't always like to talk about things, or not as explicitly as Americans (just like the exclusivity talk – that's missing for us). So, we tend to read the signs more and assume. This is exactly what I did. I assumed he and I agreed that he was not going to do it. However, as we didn't verbally or explicitly say it, he didn't think we had agreed.

Furthermore, we didn't talk about being exclusive. I assumed it and believed we were dating according to my Kissing Style (hence, we were exclusive). However, as we didn't have the exclusivity talk (according to his Hugging Style), he thought we were still in his dating phase (hence not exclusive). Therefore, according to my culture, he cheated. Based on his, he didn't.

Thomas Erikson, the author of *Surrounded by Idiots*, couldn't have phrased it better. "Communication happens on the listener's terms: Everything you say to a person is filtered through their frames of reference, biases, and preconceived ideas."

As you can see, I blame our cultural differences and misunderstandings more than I blame him, but it's the kind of misunderstanding that can be close to impossible to repair. In my culture, being exclusive from the start also implies you are serious about the person and *respect them*. Therefore, be careful if you are dating someone from the Kissing Style – don't ruin it before it starts.

## BREAKING UP

Breaking up is one of those things that seems so straightforward you might be surprised there could be misunderstandings.
In this section, to understand the differences, let's take the Hugging Style dating culture as our yardstick, just like before, simply because it is the most clearly structured.

 *Hugging Style:*

Even though it might be obvious, let's look at the three phases and their relation to breaking up.

- **Dating phase:** As you are seeing each other but not exclusive or in a relationship, parting ways doesn't count as breaking up.
- **Relationship phase:** After the exclusivity talk, once you are in a relationship, breaking up is more serious than just parting ways. It counts as a real breakup.
- **Preparing to get married:** Once you are engaged and preparing to get married, breaking up is very serious. It is calling off the wedding.

**Breaking up in the Hugging Style**

However, how we view breaking up in other dating styles is a bit different. Let's look at them.

### Kissing Style:

The big difference compared to the Hugging Style is that because the Kissing Style is automatically exclusive from the start, breaking up in the first few weeks after being exclusive is not unusual and may even be rather common. This is because even though they are exclusive, for them, this is the dating phase.

Therefore, in these few initial weeks, breaking up doesn't officially count as breaking up. You gave it a try, but if it is not working, no hard feelings. At least not for the person who is used to the Kissing Style.

KISSING

**Breaking up in the Kissing Style**

### Who will be most heartbroken after exclusivity?

However, if you are used to the Hugging Style, you will likely have already been dating for one to two months and will consider yourself to be in the relationship phase once you agree to exclusivity. Therefore, you might be very disappointed and heartbroken as, in your eyes, it was a "proper" breakup.

Those who are used to the Bowing style will likely be even more heartbroken. Let's see why.

### Bowing Style:

Those who are used to the Bowing Style will take a breakup the hardest. This is because, if you recall, going public is not only about becoming official, but it is also assumed you will get married if everything goes well. Therefore, in these cultures, breaking up is not only a relationship breakup like it is for us in Western cultures, but a more serious "calling off the wedding" type – even if no bride price/dowry had been paid yet.

BOWING

**Breaking up in the Bowing Style**

Let's look at breaking up side by side – especially how it changes after being exclusive. Please note that the Traditional Style is missing, as in those cultures, due to having arranged marriages, they do not date. Hence there is no breaking up either.

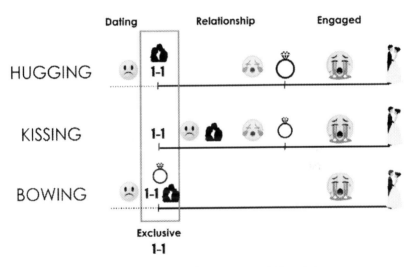

**Comparison of breaking up across dating styles**

Therefore, when you go into an intercultural relationship, consider how breaking up will affect the other person at different points in the process. A casual "parting of ways" for you might mean calling off the wedding for somebody else!

Lastly, another misunderstanding about dating is *what's OK* and *what isn't* during each stage in terms of how fast you go. So, let's compare them side by side.

| 1 | Getting to know each other (no physical contact) |
|---|---|
| 2 | Holding hands/kissing |
| 3 | Physical intimacy (sex) |
| 4 | Going on holiday together |
| 5 | Moving in together |
| 6 | Sharing finances |

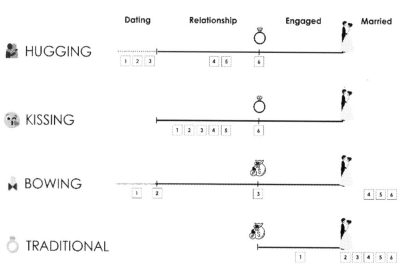

**Comparison of the timeline of dating steps**

*Assumptions:*

Even though there are three main causes of misunderstandings (language-based, behavior-based, and assumption-based, which can often be mixed), they often come down to the same thing: wrong assumptions. However, some cultures tend to assume more than others.

As we touched on above, how much we read between the lines is engraved in us: in our culture and how we communicate.
Let's look at an example.

In a YouTube video made for the Global.me 2012 project in Finland, we can see three old friends meet[cxii]:

Sisi is on a cigarette break, sitting on a bench, when Stefano walks past and greets her with great surprise.

**Stefano:** "Oooh, I want a smoke, but I forgot my cigarettes. . ."
             . . . Sisi keeps smoking.
**Stefano:** "In fact, I haven't smoked all day."
             . . . Sisi continues without taking note
**Stefano:** "You know, one cigarette would be really great."
             . . . Sisi keeps smoking.

This is when Sisi's boyfriend Antti arrives:

**Antti:** "Hi, Sweetheart!"
**Antti:** "Can I borrow a cigarette?"
**Sisi:** "Yeah, sure! Here it is!"
**Stefano:** "Oh, I also wanted a cigarette."
**Sisi:** "Why didn't you say so? It was my last one. . ."

We differentiate between two types of communication:

- **Direct (or low-context cultures):** communicating information in direct, explicit, and precise ways - just like Antti in our example.

- **Indirect (or high-context cultures):** communicating in implicit ways and relying heavily on nonverbal language – e.g., Stefano.

In countries with many immigrants (e.g., the USA and Canada), people have to communicate very clearly. They tend to be the most direct communicators.

On the other hand, when you have a long history and culture, citizens tend to assume and read each other's nonverbal communication more. Countries, especially with the Bowing Style, are very indirect, while countries with the Kissing Style tend to be halfway between direct and indirect.

| Direct | Half-direct & Indirect | Indirect |
|:---:|:---:|:---:|
| Hugging Style | Kissing Style | Bowing Style |

The more indirect/high-context a culture is, the more they are raised to read nonverbal communication and make assumptions. This also shows in their dating stages.

The **Hugging Style** is very direct and does not assume:

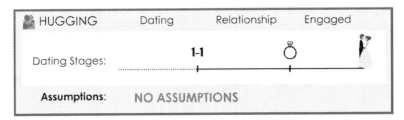

The **Kissing Style**, on the other hand, is already slightly indirect. They assume exclusivity **1-1** and the start of the relationship :

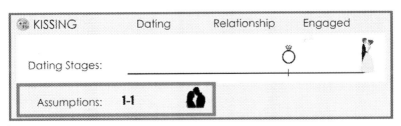

While the very indirect **Bowing Style** assumes exclusivity **1-1** and that the couple will get married (if everything goes well):

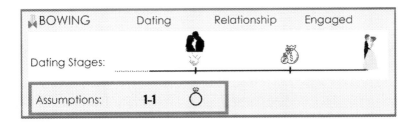

To reduce assumption-based misunderstandings, if you are used to either the Kissing or the Bowing Style, try to make a conscious effort to communicate more clearly. Validate your assumptions verbally with your partner whenever you can, especially at the beginning of the relationship.

If your partner is from the Hugging Style, they will expect things to be spelled out clearly between the two of you.

The same goes the other way around. Don't expect your partner from the Hugging Style to read between the lines. They are less likely to pick up on signals you try to imply. However, if you are used to the Kissing Style, you will need to make an extra effort to pick up on hidden signals from people with the Bowing Style. People with the Kissing Style are not as good at that as those from an Asian background; therefore, clear communication is essential.

American anthropologist Edward Hall often used the analogy of marriage to describe high- and low-context communication. In the beginning, when you are a new couple, you need to talk about every detail as you don't know your partner too well – you are direct communicators. However, after 20-30 years of marriage, you understand each other from the smallest signs, often without talking – you are now indirect communicators. This is exactly how communication differs among cultures. Countries with lots of immigrants are like a young marriage, while more traditional countries with few immigrants are like a 20-30-year marriage.

Despite direct communication being so important to avoid misunderstandings, it can also be a fine line. In Hugging Style cultures, clear and to-the-point communication is part of being a good, efficient communicator. However, in cultures that tend to read between the lines, being too direct and to the point can come across as blunt or not having class. In these cultures, being an indirect communicator is often part of having manners and being "refined," as you are good at picking up on these hidden signals. Therefore, if you are used to a clear and direct communication style in your country, try to pay attention when your partner is not comfortable with a topic – so either you can take the lead or stop talking about it.

# CHAPTER 16

# WHAT DO YOU BRING TO THE RELATIONSHIP?

## (CONCLUSION)

After nearly one year of writing, late nights, and serious coffee overdose, finally, the draft manuscript of this book was on its way to a small circle of international friends in the US, Germany, Italy, Portugal, Hungary, Ukraine etc., and last but not least, to my friend Thu in Vietnam.

After eagerly waiting for their reply, I got some amazing and extremely valuable feedback. On the other hand, I really struggled with the comments from Thu:

"I don't understand this."
"How is this related to that?"
"I can't connect the dots."

She put in so much work going through my book, and I highly appreciated her efforts, but I couldn't understand her comments.
I needed a break.

A few days later, I flew to Madeira – a Portuguese volcanic island, to speak at the *World is My Workplace* conference. With its breathtaking scenery, Madeira was the perfect break I needed.

Then. . . something clicked!

Differences in our mindsets affect every area of our life: not just dating and relationships, but something as simple as reading a book.

Western cultures think *analytically* - focusing on individual objects, while Asian cultures think *holistically* – focusing on the relationships between objects.[cxiii] Hence, while reading this book, my Western friends and I were focused on the facts, while Thu was focused on the relationships between them.

For this reason, Thu could immediately identify "holes" in the story that neither my Western friends nor I even realized were there. Sometimes, it took me serious efforts to see them, despite her pointing them out. She often suggested I move entire sections of the book to several pages or chapters earlier. That made the book much better, but I was stunned. *How did she even see that?*

Thu's culture complemented the weaknesses of mine. From that day onward, I absolutely LOVED her comments! In fact, Thu's feedback made me restructure the entire book, making sure it is easy to follow for both Westerners and Asians.

There is so much conflict in the world, but we don't realize that our cultures are complementary, like yin and yang. My analytical thinking, combined with Thu's holistic approach, made a huge difference to this book.

Intercultural relationships, just like Thu's comments, might frustrate you to the point where you even conclude it is not worth it, especially if the person's culture is very different from yours. Though, once you discover your differences, they open a whole new world. Instead of being incompatible, you become complementary. Your differences turn into your strengths and greatest assets. They make you a power couple in a way that you could never be on your own.

However, it starts by discovering yourself: by knowing what you bring to the relationship.

As Lao Tzu, the founder of philosophical Taoism, said:

"Knowing others is wisdom, knowing yourself is enlightenment."

This book is intended to help you embark on this journey. To see just how far you have come, go back and take a look at what you wrote for the exercise "What is Your Dating Style?" at the beginning of the book. How differently do you see your own culture? . . . What about others'?

We have covered a lot, and it is important for this information to sink in and to be reinstated. So, let's summarize what we have learned so far:

1. How many distinctively different dating styles exist and why.
2. How different their dating stages and mindsets are.
3. Why dating styles clash.
4. How our inheritance systems influence our dating goals: whether we date to find love or date to marry.
5. How showing or hiding our feelings affects dating in the West.
6. What the characteristics of the four distinctively different dating styles are and how there may be crossovers between them.
7. How different dating cultures may misunderstand each other, including dating, cheating, and breaking up.

You now have all the foundations to navigate the international dating scene. You have a deep understanding of the different dating styles (including consciously being aware of your own) and know the challenges you might face dating someone from another culture.

Despite all of its challenges, millions of intercultural couples around the world believe cross-cultural relationships are worth it. So, I asked several people who have been engaged or married to a foreigner how it has enriched their lives:

**Ksenia from Russia** met her Scottish husband a few years ago when they were both living in New Zealand. Ksenia shares the lessons dating a foreigner has taught her:

"The primary lesson I learned from dating a foreigner is that, fundamentally, we share more similarities than differences. Effective communication is essential to navigate potential pitfalls. Yet beneath surface-level cultural disparities, our desires remain universal: to love and be loved, to experience happiness and joy, and to be understood for who we truly are.

"Moreover, I believe it's important to see the person's individual qualities rather than their nationality. While we may hold stereotypes about people from other cultures, individuals rarely fit these narrow confines. Dating a foreigner has reinforced my belief.

"For me, the experience of dating and eventually marrying a foreigner has been overwhelmingly positive. We currently reside in his home country (the UK), and this bond has greatly helped me to adjust to my new environment."

**Chel from the USA** not only married a man from Argentina; she now even recommends Argentinian men to all her friends! She explains:

"When you are an intercultural couple, you get the opportunity to embrace the best parts of each other's culture and weave them together in the way that best suits you as a couple. I think it is really fun because there are so many creative ways to experience life, and it's really opened my perspective."

She even gives some examples from their day-to-day relationship: "My husband's culture is centered around fresh home-cooked food; I never had hand-made pasta and gnocchi in the house before I met him. But my culture prefers to eat at 7 pm, not at midnight like his." So, to embrace both cultures and make the most of them, Chel explains, "We enjoy his cuisine, but just a little bit earlier in the day!"

She also shares the positive influence her husband's culture had on her relationship with her own family in the US. "My husband's culture is very family-focused; he calls them every morning. That's made me value my own family and inspires me to connect with them daily."

**Katie from the USA** is getting married to her fiancé from Turkey.

"If you had told me that at 27, I would find my perfect partner on Bumble in a foreign country, I would have laughed. Until it happened. In February 2020, before the pandemic crept its way to Türkiye, Murat and I messaged for the first time. Three days later, we arranged our first date. The whirlwind of the next three years would teach me many things, but one is that, regardless of whether you share the most important hopes and goals for yourself in common with your partner, when you've spent your formative years in different cultures, problems can and will arise.

"There have been a few instances in the last four years, and I am sure there will be several more, but I do have to say, the benefits outweigh the difficulties. We share the same passions, we share the same love of exploration, and we have the same core values. They may have originally been in different languages, but together, we have created our own unique love language, and I wouldn't trade it for the world."

Dating a foreigner enriches many people's lives, and it often impacts their children's also! Many of them grow up bilingual and as dual citizens – which gives them a huge advantage in life. Nevertheless, intercultural dating should be fun and enjoyable, not paved with obstacles. Thus, I want to save as many people as possible from going through the same experience I had. However, I alone can't impact everyone.

That is why I started *How to Date a Foreigner*® Partner Program - a network of affiliate partners, licensed advisors, and training providers. Join other travelers, content creators, and relationship advisors who help others navigate the international dating scene and earn money by promoting *How to Date a Foreigner*® in person or on their blogs, websites, and social media.

Dating does not have to be merely a numbers game!

**Author's note:**

Thank you for reading How to Date a Foreigner!
I hope you have enjoyed it.
If you have time to spare, a short review
would be greatly appreciated.

# HOW TO DATE A FOREIGNER®
# PARTNER PROGRAM

## Affiliate Program - FREE to join. Apply today!

Loved the book? Join our Affiliate Program to earn commission for every customer you refer! When you sign up, we'll give you a unique link that you can share through your blog, website, newsletter, videos, podcast, or social media pages. You'll also have a private dashboard where you can track referrals and see your progress in real time. It's free to join. Apply today!
Go to: partners.howtodateaforeigner.com

## Become a Licensed Advisor or Training Provider

To become a licensed advisor or training provider, please visit our website: www.howtodateaforeigner.com/courses or contact us at: courses@howtodateaforeigner.com

## Further Information

For speaking opportunities and media enquiries, please email: speaking@howtodateaforeigner.com
Sylvia Halter accepts 30 speaking opportunities a year.
Please book well in advance to avoid disappointment.

# APPENDIX

# Bibliography

[i] "Census Bureau Reports 21 Percent of Married-Couple Households Have at Least One-Foreign Born Spouse" *United States Census Bureau*, last updated Sept 5, 2013, https://www.census.gov/newsroom/archives/2013-pr/cb13-157.html.

[ii] United Nations, Department of Economic and Social Affairs, Population Division, *International Migrant Stock 2020: Destination and Origin*, Table 1: International Migrant Stock at Mid-Year by Sex and by Region, Country or Area of Destination and Origin. (Original source) www.un.org/development/desa/pd/content/international-migrant-stock. Secondary Source: "Immigrant and Emigrant Populations by Country of Origin and Destination," *Migration Policy Institute*, accessed March 12, 2023, https://www.migrationpolicy.org/programs/data-hub/charts/immigrant-and-emigrant-populations-country-origin-and-destination.

[iii] China Mike, "The Cult of 'Face' in China," *China Mike*, last updated May 19, 2020, https://www.china-mike.com/chinese-culture/cult-of-face/.

[iv] William Drake, "Shame Vs Guilt: What's The Difference?," *betterhelp*, last updated January 23, 2023, https://www.betterhelp.com/advice/guilt/guilt-vs-shame-whats-the-difference-and-why-does-it-matter/.

[v] TEDx Talks, "Cross cultural communication," Pellegrino Riccardi, *TEDxBergen*, posted January 10, 2017, Youtube, 19:58, https://www.youtube.com/watch?v=yv62gqnkuso.

[vi] Richard E. Nisbett, "*The Geography of Thought: How Asians and Westerners Think Differently . . . and Why*," (Nicholas Brealey Publishing, 2005), 288.

[vii] Panayiotis Kanelos, "Learning to Argue: Ancient Greece to Today," *The Imaginative Conservative*, last updated June 26, 2019, https://theimaginativeconservative.org/2019/06/learning-argue-ancient-greece-today-panayiotis-kanelos.html.

[viii] Zhang Lihua, "China's Traditional Cultural Values and National Identity," *Carnegie Endowment for International Peace*, last updated November 21, 2013, https://carnegieendowment.org/2013/11/21/china-s-traditional-cultural-values-and-national-identity-pub-53613.

[ix] Joseph Comunale, "Islam and Sharia Law|History & Culture," *Study.com*, last updated April 14, 2022, https://study.com/learn/lesson/islam-sharia-law-history-culture.html.

[x] "What is Sharia law? What does it mean for women in Afghanistan?," *BBC*, last updated August 19, 2021, https://www.bbc.com/news/world-27307249.

xi Curtiss v. Strong, 4 Day 51 (Conn. 1809) Arnd v. Amling, 53 Md. 192 (1880);
Thurston v. Whitney, 56 Mass. 104, 110 (1848); Phebe v. Prince & Prince,
1 Miss. 131, 131 (1822); Jackson v. Griddley, 18 Johns. 98, 103 (N.Y. 1820);
Brock v. Milligan, 10 Ohio 121, 125-26 (1840). Quoted in Secondary
Source: "Judicial System," *American Atheists, accessed April 18, 2023,*
https://www.atheists.org/legal/faq/courts/.

xii Mo. Const. of 1875, art. II, § 5; Fuller v. Fuller, 17 Cal. 605, 612 (1861); Bush v.
Commonweealth, 80 Ky. 244, 250-51 (1882); Cotler v. State, 39 S.W. 576,
577 (Tex. Crim. App. 1897); Perry v. Commonwealth, 44 Va. 632 642
(1946).
Quoted in Secondary Source: "Judicial System," *American Atheists,*
*accessed April 18, 2023,* https://www.atheists.org/legal/faq/courts/.

xiii Laura Senior Primo, "The hidden rules and structure of Korean dating,"
*Korea JoongAng Daily,* last updated April 23, 2022,
https://koreajoongangdaily.joins.com/2022/04/23/national/kcampus/d
ating-kcampus/20220423070003926.html.

xiv "Gender and Land Rights Database: Bangladesh,"
*Food and Agriculture Organization of the United Nations,*
*accesse*d: February 26, 2023,
https://www.fao.org/gender-landrights-database/country-
profiles/countries-list/customary-law/en/?country_iso3=BGD.

xv "Gender and Land Rights Database: Bangladesh,"
*Food and Agriculture Organization of the United Nations,*
*accesse*d: February 26, 2023,
https://www.fao.org/gender-landrights-database/country-
profiles/countries-list/customary-law/en/?country_iso3=BGD.

xvi Britannica, T. Editors of Encyclopaedia. "patriarchy." *Encyclopedia Britannica,*
December 16, 2022. https://www.britannica.com/topic/patriarchy.

xvii Sarah Madaus "6 Matriarchal Societies That Have Been Thriving With Women
at the Helm for Centuries," *Town&Country,* last updated Aug 5, 2019,
https://www.townandcountrymag.com/society/tradition/g28565280/
matriarchal-societies-list/.

xviii "Gender and Land Rights Database: Vietnam,"
*Food and Agriculture Organization of the United Nations,*
*accesse*d: February 26, 2023,
https://www.fao.org/gender-landrights-database/country-
profiles/countries-list/customary-law/en/?country_iso3=VNM.

xix "Gender and Land Rights Database: Bangladesh,"
*Food and Agriculture Organization of the United Nations,*
*accesse*d: February 26, 2023,
https://www.fao.org/gender-landrights-database/country-
profiles/countries-list/customary-law/en/?country_iso3=BGD.

xx "Gender and Land Rights Database: Vietnam,"
*Food and Agriculture Organization of the United Nations,*
*accesse*d: February 26, 2023,
https://www.fao.org/gender-landrights-database/country-
profiles/countries-list/customary-law/en/?country_iso3=VNM.

xxi "Gender and Land Rights Database: Vietnam,"
*Food and Agriculture Organization of the United Nations,*
*access*ed: February 26, 2023,
https://www.fao.org/gender-landrights-database/country-
profiles/countries-list/customary-law/en/?country_iso3=VNM.

xxii "Gender and Land Rights Database: Bangladesh,"
*Food and Agriculture Organization of the United Nations,*
*access*ed: February 26, 2023,
https://www.fao.org/gender-landrights-database/country-
profiles/countries-list/customary-law/en/?country_iso3=BGD.

xxiii "Gender and Land Rights Database: Republic of Korea,"
*Food and Agriculture Organization of the United Nations,*
*access*ed: February 26, 2023,
https://www.fao.org/gender-landrights-database/country-
profiles/countries-list/customary-law/en/?country_iso3=KOR.

xxiv "Gender and Land Rights Database: Sri Lanka,"
*Food and Agriculture Organization of the United Nations,*
*access*ed: February 26, 2023,
https://www.fao.org/gender-landrights-database/country-
profiles/countries-list/customary-law/en/?country_iso3=LKA.

xxv "Gender and Land Rights Database: Bangladesh,"
*Food and Agriculture Organization of the United Nations,*
*access*ed: February 26, 2023,
https://www.fao.org/gender-landrights-database/country-
profiles/countries-list/customary-law/en/?country_iso3=BGD.

xxvi Sarah Madaus, "6 Matriarchal Societies that Have Been Thriving With Women
at the Helm for Centuries," *Town & Country*, published: August 5, 2019,
https://www.townandcountrymag.com/society/tradition/g28565280/
matriarchal-societies-list/.

xxvii "Gender and Land Rights Database: Bangladesh,"
*Food and Agriculture Organization of the United Nations,*
*access*ed: February 26, 2023,
https://www.fao.org/gender-landrights-database/country-
profiles/countries-list/customary-law/en/?country_iso3=BGD.

xxviii "Gender and Land Rights Database: Bangladesh,"
*Food and Agriculture Organization of the United Nations,*
*access*ed: February 26, 2023,
https://www.fao.org/gender-landrights-database/country-
profiles/countries-list/customary-law/en/?country_iso3=BGD.

xxix "Gender and Land Rights Database: Bangladesh,"
*Food and Agriculture Organization of the United Nations,*
*access*ed: February 26, 2023,
https://www.fao.org/gender-landrights-database/country-
profiles/countries-list/customary-law/en/?country_iso3=BGD.

xxx Sarah Madaus, "6 Matriarchal Societies that Have Been Thriving With Women at the Helm for Centuries," *Town & Country*, published: August 5, 2019, https://www.townandcountrymag.com/society/tradition/g28565280/matriarchal-societies-list/.

xxxi Alessandro Fais, "What's it like dating an Italian?" *Quora*, posted in 2018, https://www.quora.com/Whats-it-like-dating-an-Italian.

xxxii Paulisima, "9 Unavoidable Problems You'll Have Dating a Mexican (+How to Overcome Them)," *Spring Languages*, posted April 10, 2021, https://springlanguages.com/learn-spanish/consider-this-before-dating-a-mexican/.

xxxiii Anonymus, "How does it feel to have Chinese boyfriend?," *Quora*, posted in 2016, https://www.quora.com/How-does-it-feel-to-have-a-Chinese-boyfriend.

xxxiv "You Know You're Dating a Spanish Woman When…," *Dating Beyond Borders*, posted October 5, 2017, YouTube 4:42 https://www.youtube.com/watch?v=qjmXKYh5DlQ&t=208s.

xxxv "You Know You're Dating a Spanish Woman When…," *Dating Beyond Borders*, posted October 5, 2017, YouTube 4:42 https://www.youtube.com/watch?v=qjmXKYh5DlQ&t=208s.

xxxvi "Tips on Attracting a Chinese Woman," *Dating Beyond Borders*, posted March 8, 2019, YouTube, 9:31 https://www.youtube.com/watch?v=86X4HzGbfYQ.

xxxvii Giorgio Taietti, "Why do Italian men live with their mothers?," *Quora*, posted in 2017, https://www.quora.com/Why-do-Italian-men-live-with-their-mothers.

xxxviii Chiaki Watanabe "Are there any common rules to date Japanese guy? Well, other than you can never communicate with him during weekdays." *Quora*, posted in 2019, https://www.quora.com/Are-there-any-common-rules-to-date-Japanese-guy-Well-other-than-you-can-never-communicate-with-him-during-weekdays.

xxxix Kanan Shah, "Why do Indian parents loath the dating culture?," *Quora*, posted in 2018, https://www.quora.com/Why-do-Indian-parents-loath-the-dating-culture.

xl Ismenia Ujar "My Indian boyfriend told his parents about me after a year and a half. They were not too happy. We want to be together. He is going to keep having conversations with them. What should I do?" *Quora*, updated November 11, 2023, https://www.quora.com/My-Indian-boyfriend-told-his-parents-about-me-after-a-year-and-a-half-They-were-not-too-happy-We-want-to-be-together-He-is-going-to-keep-having-conversations-with-them-What-should-I-do.

xli Britannica, T. Editors of Encyclopaedia. "xiao."
*Encyclopedia Britannica*, February 18, 2023.
https://www.britannica.com/topic/xiao-Confucianism.

xlii "Country Comparison," *Hofstede Insights*, last accessed April 5, 2023,
https://www.hofstede-insights.com/country-comparison/the-usa/.

xliii Max Chiesa, "What is it like to date Italian women?," *Quora*, posted in 2017,
https://www.quora.com/What-is-it-like-to-date-Italian-women.

xliv "Ease of doing business rank," *The World Bank*, last updated Sept 16, 2019,
https://data.worldbank.org/indicator/IC.BUS.EASE.XQ?end=2019&start
=2019&view=map.

xlv "International Financial Statistics and data files: Lending Interest Rate (%),"
*International Monetary Fund*, accessed January 16th, 2024,
https://data.imf.org/regular.aspx?key=63087881
map via Secondary Source: Index Mundi, accessed January 16th, 2024,
https://www.indexmundi.com/facts/indicators/FR.INR.LEND.

xlvi Sebastiaan Brouwer "10 Things You Should Never Do in Spain (As a foreigner!),"
*Hola Morgan*, YouTube 15:25, posted March 12, 2021,
https://www.youtube.com/watch?v=RSShCaBZoQc&t=730s.

xlvii Netflix Series, "Sexy or Sexist?, Emily in Paris,"
*Netflix*, Season 1 Episode 3, 25:28

xlviii Oscar Terrazas, "How do dating and relationships work in Mexico?"
Quora, posted in 2015,
https://www.quora.com/How-do-dating-and-relationships-work-in-
Mexico.

xlix "Hand-kissing," *Wikipedia*, last updated March 22, 2023,
https://en.wikipedia.org/wiki/Hand-kissing.

l "Eye-Gazing: this simple exercise CHANGES your relationship," *ikario*,
posted April 29, 2021, YouTube, 8:27,
https://www.youtube.com/watch?v=uDW-tp4Jzhk&t=9s.

li "Every dating dynamic ever," *Ana Akana*,
posted January 20, 2021, YouTube, 33:00,
https://www.youtube.com/watch?v=jSj9ulKsPLA.

lii Robert Greene, "The Art of Seduction," Narrator: Joseph Powers
(HighBridge, a division of Recorded Books, 2015), Audiobook, 22:51 min.

liii TEDx Talks, "The power of seduction in our everyday lives," Chen Lizra,
*TEDxVancouver*, posted February 1, 2013, YouTube, 12:47,
https://www.youtube.com/watch?v=TBIL2sdfoVc.

liv Camille Chevalier-Karfis, "French Women Don't Date: The French Dating
System Explained," *Frenchtoday*, updated June 7, 2021,
https://www.frenchtoday.com/blog/french-culture/french-dating-
system-explained/.

[lv] Rebecca Dossantos, "5 Dating Differences between Americans and Europeans," *Pimsleur*, accessed March 12, 2023, https://blog.pimsleur.com/2020/02/14/dating-differences-between-americans-and-europeans/.

[lvi] Debora Nery, "10 Tips for Dating a Brazillian Girl for Gringos," Tim Explica, YouTube 6:52, posted in 2019, https://www.youtube.com/watch?v=WyQDhwF1ZRM.

[lvii] Melanie Pollock, "French Dating Etiquette," *Talkinfrench*, updated August 29, 2022, https://www.talkinfrench.com/french-dating-etiquette/.

[lviii] Haruna Miyamoto-Borg, LCSW, "Culture Shapes How We Behave in the Dating Process," *Psychology Today*, last updated April 14, 2019, https://www.psychologytoday.com/us/blog/couples-and-culture/201904/culture-shapes-how-we-behave-in-the-dating-process.

[lix] Anonymus, "How does it feel to have Chinese boyfriend?," *Quora*, posted in 2016, https://www.quora.com/How-does-it-feel-to-have-a-Chinese-boyfriend.

[lx] RePENT_22, "three day rule," *Urban Dictionary*, last updated May 8, 2007, https://www.urbandictionary.com/define.php?term=three%20day%20rule.

[lxi] Jonathon Aslay, "How Many Dates It Takes For A Guy To Get Serious About A Relationship?," *YourTango*, last modified Oct 1, 2021, https://www.yourtango.com/experts/jonathon-aslay/why-10-date-rule-works.

[lxii] Mariana Albuquerque, "You Know You're Dating a Brazillian Woman When..." *Dating Beyond Borders*, posted in 2016, https://www.youtube.com/watch?v=FKcmM2j1AJU.

[lxiii] Netflix Series, "The Cook, the Thief, Her Ghost and His Lover, Emily in Paris," *Netflix*, Season 2 Episode 7, 28:10

[lxiv] Alessia S., "What it is like dating an Italian man?" *Quora*, posted in 2018, https://www.quora.com/What-is-it-like-dating-an-Italian-man.

[lxv] Mikulincer, M., Shaver, P.R. & Pereg, D., "Attachment Theory and Affect Regulation: The Dynamics, Development, and Cognitive Consequences of Attachment-Related Strategies." *Motivation and Emotion* **27**, 77–102 (2003). https://doi.org/10.1023/A:1024515519160.

[lxvi] Mikulincer, M., Shaver, P.R. & Pereg, D., "Attachment Theory and Affect Regulation: The Dynamics, Development, and Cognitive Consequences of Attachment-Related Strategies." *Motivation and Emotion* **27**, 77–102 (2003). https://doi.org/10.1023/A:1024515519160.

lxvii Danielle Emma, "Attachment Styles & Relationship Hurdles," The Love List, Last updated August 21, 2020, https://thelovelist.org/2020/08/21/attachment-styles-relationship-hurdles/.

lxviii Mikulincer, M., Shaver, P.R. & Pereg, D., "Attachment Theory and Affect Regulation: The Dynamics, Development, and Cognitive Consequences of Attachment-Related Strategies." *Motivation and Emotion* **27**, 77–102 (2003). https://doi.org/10.1023/A:1024515519160.

lxix Mikulincer, M., Shaver, P.R. & Pereg, D., "Attachment Theory and Affect Regulation: The Dynamics, Development, and Cognitive Consequences of Attachment-Related Strategies." *Motivation and Emotion* **27**, 77–102 (2003). https://doi.org/10.1023/A:1024515519160.

lxx Camille Chevalier-Karfis, "French Women Don't Date: The French Dating System Explained," *Frenchtoday*, updated June 7, 2021, https://www.frenchtoday.com/blog/french-culture/french-dating-system-explained/.

lxxi Faye James, "How soon is too soon to say 'I love you'?," *Body+Soul*, published July 2, 2019, https://www.bodyandsoul.com.au/sex-relationships/how-soon-is-too-soon-to-say-i-love-you/news-story/a85676baf5db73a46828002499634388.

lxxii Anonymus, "How long does it usually take to say 'I love you' to girlfriend or boyfriend?," *Reddit*, published December 11, 2021, https://www.reddit.com/r/AskAnAmerican/comments/rdynym/how_l ong_does_it_usually_takes_to_say_i_love_you/.

lxxiii "Why Foreign Women Struggle Dating in Japan," *TAKASHii from Japan*, posted December 7, 2022, YouTube 13:48, https://www.youtube.com/watch?v=JTifbDPZEE8.

lxxiv Debacchatio, "Do Brazilians say 'I love you' sooner when dating than Americans?," *Reddit*, published October 2, 2022, https://www.reddit.com/r/Brazil/comments/xthw03/do_brazilians_say _i_love_you_sooner_when_dating/.

lxxv Camille Chevalier-Karfis, "French Women Don't Date: The French Dating System Explained," *Frenchtoday*, updated June 7, 2021, https://www.frenchtoday.com/blog/french-culture/french-dating-system-explained/.

lxxvi Sylvia Sabes, "Why the French rarely say 'I love you'," *BBC*, posted June 14, 2021, https://www.bbc.com/travel/article/20210613-why-the-french-rarely-say-i-love-you.

lxxvii Lorna S. Wei, "No bride price, no marriage in China," *Think China*, last updated November 20, 2019, https://www.thinkchina.sg/no-bride-price-no-marriage-china.

lxxviii Norimitsu Onishi, "In South Korea, tying the knot has plenty of strings attached," *The New York Times*, last updated March 21, 2007, https://www.nytimes.com/2007/03/21/world/asia/21iht-dowry.4983084.html.

lxxix Mustika Hapsoro, "South Korea is Giving Men Money to Buy a Bride to Save Its Shrinking Population," *Vice*, last updated February 19, 2019, https://www.vice.com/en/article/xwbvyd/south-korea-shrinking-population-marriage-subsidy.

lxxx Mami Suzuki, "Kokuhaku: Japan's Love Confessing Culture," *ToFuGu*, published October 23, 2013, https://www.tofugu.com/japan/kokuhaku-love-confessing-japan/.

lxxxi Mami Suzuki, "Kokuhaku: Japan's Love Confessing Culture," *ToFuGu*, published October 23, 2013, https://www.tofugu.com/japan/kokuhaku-love-confessing-japan/.

lxxxii Chris Lynd, "'Be My Girlfriend': Eccentric Taiwanese Dating Culture," *Taida Journal*, published April 13, 2020, https://taidajournal.tumblr.com/post/615214168416665600/be-my-girlfriend-eccentric-taiwanese-dating.

lxxxiii Choi Jae-hee, "Quirks of Korean dating explained," *The Korean Herald*, published May 16,2022, https://www.koreaherald.com/view.php?ud=20220516000687.

lxxxiv Duc Nguyen, "How does Vietnamese courtship work?" *Quora*, published in 2016, https://www.quora.com/How-does-Vietnamese-courtship-work?top_ans=27243268.

lxxxv Mami Suzuki, "Kokuhaku: Japan's Love Confessing Culture," *ToFuGu*, published October 23, 2013, https://www.tofugu.com/japan/kokuhaku-love-confessing-japan/.

lxxxvi Mami Suzuki, "Kokuhaku: Japan's Love Confessing Culture," *ToFuGu*, published October 23, 2013, https://www.tofugu.com/japan/kokuhaku-love-confessing-japan/.

lxxxvii Chris Lynd, "'Be My Girlfriend': Eccentric Taiwanese Dating Culture," *Taida Journal*, published April 13, 2020, https://taidajournal.tumblr.com/post/615214168416665600/be-my-girlfriend-eccentric-taiwanese-dating.

lxxxviii Interesting_Carrot26, "How long does it usually take to say 'I love you' to girlfriend or boyfriend?," *Reddit*, published December 11, 2021, https://www.reddit.com/r/AskAnAmerican/comments/rdynym/how_long_does_it_usually_takes_to_say_i_love_you/.

lxxxix "Arab Cultural Awareness: 58 Factsheets," *Office of the Deputy Chief of Staff for Intelligence US Army Training and Doctrine Command*, FT. Leavenworth, Kansas, last updated January, 2006, https://irp.fas.org/agency/army/arabculture.pdf.

xc "Do Arranged Marriages Still Happen in 2019?," *New Idea*,
    Last updated August 2, 2019,
    https://www.newidea.com.au/arranged-marriage-is-it-the-same-as-a-
    forced-marriage.

xci Mohsina Saqlaini "Is romance allowed in Islam?," *Quora*,
    last updated 4 years ago (2019),
    https://qr.ae/prGWhB.

xcii ABC News In-depth, "Saudis have been Abandoning their Kids Abroad,
    Now the Children want Answers" *Foreign Correspondent*,
    posted May 19, 2022, Youtube, 29:31,
    https://www.youtube.com/watch?v=qLidxfL8q1Q.

xciii "Nikkah in the UK," *Milson Legal Solicitors*, last updated January 9, 2017,
    http://milsonlegalsolicitors.uk/2017/01/09/nikkah-in-the-uk/.

xciv Mehmet Paksu, "Is the money taken under the name of mahr (dowry) in Islam
    the same as bride price? What is the criterion in mahr?,"
    *Questions on Islam*, accessed March 11, 2023,
    https://questionsonislam.com/article/money-taken-under-name-mahr-
    dowry-islam-same-bride-price-what-criterion-mahr.

xcv Mehmet Paksu, "How should engagement and the period of engagement be?
    What should the criterion for the engaged couple to meet each other
    be?," *Questions on Islam*, accessed March 11, 2023,
    https://questionsonislam.com/article/how-should-engagement-and-
    period-engagement-be-what-should-criterion-engaged-couple-meet.

xcvi Mostafa Hassan, "Is it forbidden for unmarried Muslim man and woman to
    kiss?" *Quora*, last updated 5 years ago (2018), https://qr.ae/prGWrP.

xcvii "India Today," Volume 19, Issues 13-18, *Thomson Living Media India Ltd.*, 1994
    https://books.google.hu/books?redir_esc=y&id=oXBDAAAAYAAJ&fo
    cus=searchwithinvolume&q=dinners,

xcviii "Indian Anthropologist: Journal of the Indian Anthropological Association,"
    Volume 4, *Indian Anthropological Association* (1974)
    https://books.google.hu/books?redir_esc=y&id=IJgrAAAAIAAJ&focus
    =searchwithinvolume&q=pre-marital+courtship,

xcix "Forced marriage," *Wikipedia*, last updated March 13, 2023,
    https://en.wikipedia.org/wiki/Forced_marriage.

c "Dowry System in India," *Wikipedia*, last updated Feb 3, 2023,
    https://en.wikipedia.org/wiki/Dowry_system_in_India.

ci "Married for a Minute," *BBC*, first aired on the BBC on May 13, 2013,
    https://www.bbc.co.uk/programmes/b01sdpfp.

cii Asya "Are Relationships & Dating Haram in Islam?,"
    *Halal Guidance*, accessed May 12, 2023,
    https://halalguidance.com/are-relationships-dating-haram-in-islam/.

ciii P.K. Abdul Ghafour, "Temporary Marriages with Indonesian Women on the Rise," *Arab News*, last updated April 18, 2009, https://www.arabnews.com/node/323345.

civ Neha Rashid, "How Young Muslims Define 'Halal Dating' for Themselves," *NPR*, last updated April 20, 2017, https://www.npr.org/sections/codeswitch/2017/04/20/502461218/how-young-muslims-define-halal-dating-for-themselves?t=1651493874889.

cv Jonathon Ashlay, "How Many Dates It Takes For A Guy To Get Serious About A Relationship," *Yourtango*, last updated Oct 1, 2021, https://www.yourtango.com/experts/jonathon-aslay/why-10-date-rule-works.

cvi Jakob Kidde Sauntved, "What does 'Swedish style' mean dating wise?" *Quora,* posted in 2019, https://www.quora.com/What-does-Swedish-style-mean-dating-wise.

cvii Johanna Appelberg, "What is dating in Sweden like?" *Quora*, posted in 2018, https://www.quora.com/What-is-dating-in-Sweden-like.

cviii "'Buying' your fiancé for marriage?," *Japan Guide*, posted June 10, 2007, https://www.japan-guide.com/forum/quereadisplay.html?0+36835.

cix Nathan, "The Art of Proposing to a Japanese Girl," *TOFOGU*, last updated December 19, 2013, https://www.tofugu.com/japan/proposing-to-a-japanese-girl/.

cx David Kwalimwa, "Can't afford bride price? Japan is the place to be," *Nairobi News*, last modified August 19, 2015, https://nairobinews.nation.africa/cant-afford-bride-price-japan-is-the-place-to-be/.

cxi Created with MapChart, https://www.mapchart.net.

cxii Andrej Cernik, "Direct Vs Indirect communication," *Global.me*, posted September 13, 2012, YouTube, 2:33, https://www.youtube.com/watch?v=korMB9shjC4.

cxiii Andrei Lux, "Are you a more Holistic or Analytical Thinker? Take This Quiz to Find Out," *Ethical Systems*, last modified December 29, 2021, https://www.ethicalsystems.org/are-you-a-more-holistic-or-analytic-thinker-take-this-quiz-to-find-out.